READER REVI1

Any serious Budo enthusiast would be wise to have this book. The author is a long time budoka that I met in Japan and we have remained connected through our shared love of Budo and true practice. This book will enhance the understanding of "practice" on many levels.

— CHUCK CLARK [FOUNDER, JIYUSHIN-RYU AIKIBUDO]

"The Language of Aikido"... is a well-researched book steeped with scholarship, personal experience, and heart. I believe "The Language of Aikido" will help clarify the Japanese language as used in Aikido to deepen both the theory and practice of our art for practitioners of our art. An invaluable addition to every Aikido library. Highly recommended!

— JUN AKIYAMA [AIKIWEB.COM]

This is a book all Aikido people will want to read cover to cover, probably more than once. It is a detailed reference work, and also human and readable. Not only is it well-written, it's also beautifully formatted. I don't say this lightly: this book is going to be an instant classic that every student of the art should own.

— LINDA ESKIN [GRABMYWRIST.COM]

Wonderful for the novice or expert.

— HOWARD POPKIN [GINJUKAI]

I highly recommend this book for a better contextual translation of the Japanese words and characters as applies to the practice of all the various forms of Aikido, Aikibudo, and so forth. There is also a great sampling of history and Aikido nomenclature from different schools and related Budo studies. It allows the student to consider multiple viewpoints and translations of frequently used terms in our practice as they develop their own knowledge and authority in their practice.

— TARIK GHBEISH [IWAE DOJO]

Students, teachers, or anyone interested in Aikido or Budo should absolutely be adding this to their library. I learned a surprising amount from this book.

— PHIL EYERS [GENRYUKAN AIKIDO]

As a student of Japanese Budo since the age of nine, I have always searched for good books to supplement my training and to enhance my understanding. Over the years, I have noticed that they tend to fall into one of 2 major categories once on the bookshelf: entertainment and references. The vast majority make up the former. After reading the Kindle version of "The Language of Aikido," I am certain that I will have more than one hard copy if only to have an extra to loan. This is the book that I wish I would have had access to when I was a youngster struggling to grasp the subtleties of my training.

— JASON MOKRY [MOKURIN DOJO]

I studied Japanese and Aikido while living in Japan, and I only wish I'd had this book up my gi-sleeve to help me put it all together. Michael's work is concise with just enough Linguistic Nerd Sauce thrown in for those of us with a deeper background in the language to want to find our old text books to refresh our internal lexicons.

If you study Aikido (or any Japanese based art) and want to know more about the language that goes with it, this is the best place to begin your linguistic journey.

— CHARLES CHARBENEAU

Proud of you Michael!

— LYNNE HACKER [MICHAEL'S MOTHER]

THE LANGUAGE OF AIKIDO

A PRACTITIONER'S GUIDE TO JAPANESE
CHARACTERS AND TERMINOLOGY

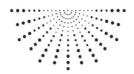

MICHAEL J. HACKER

CONTENTS

THE LANGUAGE OF AIKIDŌ

A Practitioner's Guide to Japanese Characters and Terminology

Michael J. Hacker, M.A.
TalkingBudo.com

The Language of Aikidō: A Practitioner's Guide to Japanese Characters and Terminology

© 2017 Michael J. Hacker, M.A.

DEDICATION

To my teachers, colleagues, and students. Without you, I might never have known that there was a need for such a book.

To my grandparents, Clara and George Hacker, neither of whom likely even knew I was interested in this stuff at all.

To my step grandfather Gary Brown, who passed from this world on the very day I finished writing.

To my parents, Lynne and Ted Hacker, who nurtured my curiosity, then let me go when it was time to start my journey into the void.

And finally, to Swan, who put up with me for the entire almost-decade it took me to write this. It would not have been possible without you.

「合気とは愛である」Aiki is Love.

— UESHIBA MORIHEI 植芝盛平

FOREWORD

日本の武道は、全世界に広まり、空手道、柔道、剣道、そして合気道
と、様々な武道の修行をされる方々を、多く見られるようになりまし
た、日本の武道を学ぶ行程において、技の動きを習得すると共に、技
の名称から始まり、礼儀作法用語 、道場内必要用語、一般武道用語
等、多くの日本語を理解する事も重要な課題とされています、

この度、長年合気道の修行をされ、日本語を研究されたMichael
Hacker 氏が、合気道修業者を対象に 『The Language of Aikido 』を
出版されました、この書籍が、合気道をはじめ、多くの日本武道を修
業される方々の為に、武道一般必要用語理解への ˋ道しるべˋ として
活用して頂ける事を願っております、

池田裕
合気道師範 七段
米国コロラド州ボルダー合気会創設者

With the spread of Japanese martial arts all over the world, I have
come to encounter many people who practice various arts such as

Karate, Jūdō, Kendō, and Aikidō. In the process of learning these arts, in addition to learning technical movement, understanding the Japanese language is important—starting with necessary words for use in the dojo including the names of techniques, etiquette-related phrases, practice terminology, and general martial arts vocabulary.

Michael Hacker, who has studied both the Japanese language and Aikidō for many years, has published "The Language of Aikidō" for students of the art. It is my hope that students of Aikidō and other Japanese martial arts will find this book useful as a guide for better understanding the language used in Japanese Budō.

Ikeda Hiroshi
Aikikai Shihan 7th Dan
Boulder Aikikai Founder and Chief Instructor

ACKNOWLEDGMENTS

Thanks to Carol Shifflett for talking me into writing this book in the first place (revenge is sweet) and to all of my friends for keeping me sane(ish) during the writing process. Finishing this book took far, far longer than I could've ever foreseen. Had I known how long it might end up taking, I'm not sure I'd have even begun. Sometimes, ignorance really is bliss.

Thanks to Jun Akiyama for the decades of friendship, training, conversation, shared meals, linguistic assistance, and guidance. Had you not kicked me in the butt when I most needed it (which was often), this book would never have escaped the outline stage.

Thanks to Tarik Ghbeish and Amanda Ambrosio for their inquisitiveness; without it, this book would likely be even more incomplete than it is.

I am especially indebted to my beta-readers, regardless of the amount of feedback they gave. While I can't mention everyone by name, I'd be remiss if I didn't thank Aaron Clark, Dr. Peter Goldsbury, Andrew Wilson, Kyle Davis, Philip Akin, Peter Boylan, Kjartan Clausen, Erik Jensen, Dale Matthews, Phil Eyers, Linda Eskin, and the inimitable

Janet Rosen. Thank you for helping me trudge through some especially awkward stages by giving the rough manuscript a good once-over, providing much-needed feedback, or just plain ol' distracting me with bad puns long enough for me to get my head back on track.

Special technical advisory credit goes to C. E. Clark (Founder, Jiyūshin-ryū Aikibudō and my own teacher), Dr. Karl Friday (Menkyo Kaiden of Kashima Shin-ryū), Ellis Amdur (licensed instructor in Araki-ryū Torite-Kogusoku and Toda-ha Bukō-ryū), Tobin Threadgill (Menkyo Kaiden and Kaichō, Takamura-ha Shindō Yōshin-ryū), and Howard Popkin (Daito Ryu Aikijujitsu Ginjukai) for sharing their perspectives on various topics.

My eternal gratitude goes out to all my Jiyūshinkai sisters and brothers for teaching me their (our) strange, wonderful ways and for adopting me as one of the tribe.

Finally, Double Secret Probation Thanks to Swan. *I finally did it.*

INTRODUCTION

In addition to having had the great fortune to spend 10 years living, working, and training in Japan, I have also been blessed with an apparent affinity for picking up languages. This has, it turns out, proven somewhat beneficial to me. However, throughout the years, I've heard many of my less linguistically-inclined fellow English-speaking Aiki practitioners struggle, on occasion, with the Japanese terminology associated with their chosen art.

Some people I have talked to about this subject have even gone so far as to suggest that knowledge of Japanese is not only irrelevant, but that it can and should be completely replaced by whatever native language one happens to speak. While I certainly sympathize with this notion, I do not agree with it. This book is my attempt to explain, as much as possible, why I feel this way.

Japanese kanji (characters), unlike most Western writing systems with which you are likely familiar, are quite visually rich in nature and can represent entire concepts and, in some cases, contain a multitude of meanings. As such, once understood, they give a certain flavor to words that mere sounds and letters alone can't quite manage. Even a very basic knowledge of these characters, while definitely not a prerequisite for Aikidō training, can only help to enrich one's journey.

In this book, I present the reader with some fairly rudimentary information regarding the history and composition of kanji followed by examples of many of the Japanese characters used in Aikidō terminology. Also, in order to offer a fuller appreciation of the flavors of each character, I will—on occasion—present some examples of different ways that Aikidō-related kanji are used in everyday colloquial Japanese.

Throughout this book, I have chosen to render pronunciations in *italics*, immediately following the kanji they represent. Where I have thought it useful, I have included a character-by-character breakdown in English written in square brackets [...] which represents a more literal word-for-word translation of the characters involved.

My purpose is not to teach you how to speak or read contemporary Japanese, nor should this book necessarily be seen as a replacement for your dōjō's glossary. Even among native speakers and different groups throughout Japan, there is often disagreement as to what certain words mean or which characters or terminology is "correct." Add to that the usual issues related to translation from one language to another, and the problems compound. Please consult your teacher or seniors for what language is considered correct in your particular dōjō or lineage.

Something I have chosen not to do in this book is to provide every possible 音読み *on yomi* (Chinese) and 訓読み *kun yomi* (Japanese) reading for each kanji. Not only would this have unnecessarily increased the size of this book, I don't feel that doing so would've been very useful; those multitudinous pronunciations don't tend to find their way into day-to-day dōjō Japanese and might've proven even more confusing to the reader.

Ultimately, my goal is to help non-Japanese-speaking Aikidō practitioners see meaningful messages in the characters instead of just random lines and squiggles. It is my sincere hope that this book will help you along your path by making some of the linguistic aspects of your art more easily understandable and possibly even enjoyable.

With the late Saitō Morihiro sensei, my teachers Amanō Shigeko (to Saitō sensei's left) and Shinō Masakatsu (to Saitō sensei's right), and friends at the Aiki Jinja in Iwama, Japan sometime in the early-mid 90s. I am in the rear, between Saitō and Amanō sensei.

Note to the reader: The first two chapters of this book are designed to give you some very basic linguistic background information on two aspects of the Japanese language:

Chapter one explores the basics of Japanese pronunciation and syllabaries. Chapter two takes a deeper look at how Japanese characters are constructed so that you can, hopefully, learn to decipher them more easily.

While I have endeavored to make these chapters as easily digestible as possible for the non-linguist, I realize that the material may be a little excessive for some. If you are solely interested in looking at how different terms and names are rendered in kanji, feel free to skip these first two chapters. Doing so shouldn't hinder you. They'll always be there waiting for you, should you decide to dig in later.

Finally, although I have painstakingly attempted to make sure this book is as error-free as possible, there will inevitably be mistakes and omissions. The responsibility for these oversights is mine alone. Should you happen to find any such errors or feel that I left out something important, I can be reached through the contact page on my website: talkingbudo.com. If I use your feedback in subsequent editions, I will give you full credit (unless you request otherwise). I look forward to hearing from you.

頑張って!

Michael J. Hacker, M.A.
Chandler, Arizona

PRONUNCIATION

Vowels

Just as there is more than one way to skin the proverbial cat, there is more than one way to Romanize Japanese. Rather than use 日本式ローマ字 *nihon-shiki rōmaji* Japan-style Romanization or 訓令式ローマ字 *kunrei-shiki rōmaji*, a government-ordered Romanization system supported by the Japanese Ministry of Education, I have opted to use ヘボン式ローマ字 *hebon-shiki rōmaji* Hepburn-style Romanization (in *italics*), slightly modified to help the English-speaking learner. I've chosen to do so because I feel it closer mimics the phonology of Japanese in a way that is more easily grasped by English speakers.

Japanese pronunciation is relatively easy to learn. One key is to avoid the temptation to pronounce it the way you would pronounce your own language (unless, of course, your native language is Japanese). Let's begin with the vowels. At first glance, they appear to be similar to the familiar 5 English vowels (a, e, i, o, and u), but the order is different and, unlike English, each vowel basically has only one sound. Because of this fact, Japanese vowels don't tend to throw too many curveballs at the language learner.

あ	い	う	え	お
a	i	u	e	o
f**a**ther	f**ee**t	s**oo**n	s**e**t	**o**ld

Note: Japanese vowels sound very similar to Spanish vowels.

Although groups of English vowels often result in diphthongs (i.e., one vowel "slides" into the next), Japanese vowels tend to produce more distinct phonemes. What this means is that they don't blend together quite the way they do in English. For example, the word *mae* (front) is pronounced *ma-e*, not *may* or *my*. The word *aoi* (blue) is pronounced *a-o-i*. That said, the sounds can sometimes sound smooshed together.

Depending on the dialect and circumstances, *-i* and *-u* can sometimes be "swallowed" a bit. For instance, the family name *Yamashita* is not pronounced *ya-ma-shéet-a*, but rather *ya-má-sh'ta*. In the case of final *su* (e.g., in the copula です *desu*), the final vowel is barely pronounced at all (i.e. *des'*). In Tokyo, the native Japanese word for one (thing), *hitotsu*, can sound almost like *sh'tots'*. *Futatsu* (two things) can be pronounced *f'tats'*. Unfortunately, I think the only way to *really* learn all of the ins, outs, and exceptions is to spend a great deal of time traveling around Japan and listening to the various dialects. However, since a complete treatise on Japanese phonology is outside the scope of this book, I won't dwell on it much.

To Stress... or Not to Stress?

A common problem I have noticed, especially with Americans and Brits trying to pronounce Japanese, is the insertion of unneeded stress on words or the placement of stress on the inc*orr*ect syll*a*ble. For example, just as the female name *Akiko* is *not* pronounced *uh-KEY-koh*, *Aikidō* is *not* pronounced *uh-KEY-doh*. Remember that vowels basically have one pronunciation and do not generally become unstressed like in English. Because this is not a Japanese phonology textbook, I'll just give you a very simple (perhaps overly simplistic) rule of thumb: don't add extra stress to syllables. Try to pronounce each syllable as evenly as possible. Until you can immerse yourself in a Japanese-speaking environment and soak up the intricacies yourself, it may be better to not stress yourself out over stress.

If you remember nothing else... please remember this. There is no *uh* sound in the standard Tōkyō dialect of Japanese. No *kuhratty*. No *uhkeedo*. (And, for God's sake, never say *carry-okey*.)

~

Syllabaries

Before we go into detail regarding consonants, it might be useful to introduce the concept of a *syllabary*, as Japanese has neither an alphabet nor separate consonants like English does. Omniglot defines a syllabary as "a phonetic writing system consisting of symbols representing syllables ... often made up of a consonant plus a vowel or a single vowel." Since Japanese—with the exception of the final *-n* sound—has no independent consonants, we first need to explore the native Japanese syllabaries.

Throughout the book, you may occasionally notice the use of cursive-like characters that appear to be much simpler than kanji. These characters are called 平仮名 *hiragana*; they are used to visually express syllables. Sometimes, they are used to indicate the pronunciation of rare or hard-to-read kanji or as a phonetic guide (振仮名 *furigana*) for children (who are generally unable to read kanji at a young age). In this book, I'm primarily using them as 送り仮名 *okurigana*, or syllables used after kanji to complete the full reading of a word or to indicate grammatical features. As we press on, you'll see what I mean by that.

Although I mentioned syllables, in the case of Japanese, it may be better to think in terms of *morae* instead. Simply put, a *mora* is a phonological unit; in Japanese, a syllable can contain more than one mora. If you have musical inclinations, thinking of a 2-mora vowel as taking up 2 "beats" might help.

It is generally easier to visualize morae when one writes in hiragana than in ローマ字 *Rōmaji* (Roman letters). For example, while the word Aikidō may have 3 pronounced syllables (ai-ki-dō) from the standpoint of an English speaker, it actually comprises 5 morae (あいきどう) a-i-ki-do-u. Instead of following the hiragana strictly, I have opted to use a ˉ (macron) over the letter "o" to indicate that it represents 2 morae (that is, it is elongated as in *o-u* or *o-o*, whichever the case may be). This should result in a spelling that is more familiar to the English-speaking eye. *Aikidō* and *Tōkyō* are, I think, much easier on the optics than *Aikidou* and *Toukyou*.

Japanese uses a system of syllabic organization called 五十音 *gojūon* or "fifty sounds." It's quite logically laid out, and not hard at all to memorize. If you can remember the phrase, "All Kanji Symbols, Take Note How Much You Read (and) Write," and the order of the vowels (a, i, u, e, o), you can remember how the hiragana are organized.

There is another, more angular-looking syllabary called 片仮名 *katakana* which maps directly to the hiragana syllables; it is used to render foreign loan words (e.g. マクドナルド *ma-ku-do-na-ru-do* McDonald's, グーグル *gū-gu-ru* Google, アメリカ *a-me-ri-ka* America, etc.) and in other ways similar to how we use *italics* in English for emphasis. This syllabary is, with little exception, outside the scope of this book and will thus not be covered further.

Consonant+Vowel Combinations

For the most part, the consonant portions of consonant+vowel combinations are pronounced pretty similarly to English. One notable exception is *fu* (a voiceless bilabial fricative in phonological terms). To make this sound, round your lips and lightly expel air like you're blowing out a candle on a birthday cake. Another exception is r- (an apical postalveolar flap for the linguists out there). I still find it a bit strange that we Romanize this sound as r because it does not actually represent the English "r" sound at all, but rather something akin to a hybrid of an l, an r, and a d. It is written as [ɺ] in the International Phonetic Alphabet (IPA) .

The following table shows unvoiced consonant+vowel syllables (for k-, s-, t-, and h-). *Unvoiced* means that the larynx is not vibrating when you produce the sound. *Voiced* means that the larynx vibrates. For example, place your fingers on your throat and say **k** (unvoiced), followed by **g** (voiced). Do you feel the difference?

a	i	u	e	o
あ	い	う	え	お

ka	ki	ku	ke	ko
か	き	く	け	こ

sa	shi	su	se	so
さ	し	す	せ	そ

ta	chi	tsu	te	to
た	ち	つ	て	と

na	ni	nu	ne	no
な	に	ぬ	ね	の

ha	hi	fu	he	ho
は	ひ	ふ	へ	ほ

ma	mi	mu	me	mo
ま	み	む	め	も

ya		yu		yo
や		ゆ		よ

ra	ri	ru	re	ro
ら	り	る	れ	ろ

wa	wi		we	wo
わ	ゐ		ゑ	を

-n
ん

Unvoiced Consonants

Note that in the i position, s and t change. There is no si or ti sound in Japanese, rather shi and chi. Also, there is no tu, but rather tsu.

ga	gi	gu	ge	go
が	ぎ	ぐ	げ	ご

za	ji	zu	ze	zo
ざ	じ	ず	ず	ぞ

da	dji	dzu	de	do
だ	ぢ	づ	で	ど

ba	bi	bu	be	bo
ば	び	ぶ	べ	ぼ

pa	pi	pu	pe	po
ぱ	ぴ	ぷ	ぺ	ぽ

Voiced Consonants

There are also other vowel combinations that need to be made, but which aren't represented as single vowel characters. These *palatalized* sounds happen with most consonants in the *a*, *u*, and *o* positions and are represented with a half-sized や *ya*, ゆ *yu*, and よ *yo*.

kya	kyu	kyo
きゃ	きゅ	きょ

sha	shu	sho
しゃ	しゅ	しょ

cha	chu	cho
ちゃ	ちゅ	ちょ

nya	nyu	nyo
にゃ	にゅ	にょ

hya	hyu	hyo
ひゃ	ひゅ	ひょ

mya	myu	myo
みゃ	みゅ	みょ

rya	ryu	ryo
りゃ	りゅ	りょ

gya	gyu	gyo
ぎゃ	ぎゅ	ぎょ

ja	ju	jo
じゃ	じゅ	じょ

bya	byu	byo
びゃ	びゅ	びょ

pya	pyu	pyo
ぴゃ	ぴゅ	ぴょ

Palatalized Sounds

Another important thing to note is *sequential voicing*. When this occurs, the voicing of an initial consonant in a non-initial position can change, depending on circumstances. If you're not a linguist, I don't expect you to understand exactly what that means, so here are a few examples:

/k→g/

kote + kaeshi → kote*g*aeshi [forearm + return]

/s→z/

san + sen → san*z*en [three + thousand = 3,000]

/t→d/

ran + tori → ran*d*ori [chaos + take = randori]

/n→b/

san + hyaku → sa*mb*yaku [three + hundred = 300]

As seen in *san+hyaku*, the final *-n* can also change to an *-m* sound when followed by *p-, b-,* and *m-*.

sen + hai → se*mp*ai [before + comrade = senior/elder]

hon + bu → ho*m*bu [main + bureau = headquarters]

gan + haru → ga*mb*aru = [stubborn + spread/stretch] = to do persevere; to do one's best]

One last phonological construct I'll cover here is the geminate, or "doubled" consonant. In hiragana, this is written by using a small *tsu* (っ), followed by the consonant (+vowel) to be doubled. This creates sort of a pause between the start and finish of the consonant sound. For example, bo*kk*en would be written ぼっけん. Notice how the っ is half-sized?

Note that i*kk*yō (一教) is correct, while ni*kk*yō is not. This is because the final sound (ち *chi*) in the first kanji (一 *ichi*) in ikkyō, followed by the initial *k* sound in the second kanji (教 *kyō*) requires a change from -chi to the geminate, but the final sound of the first kanji of nikyō (二 *ni*) does not. A full examination of the grammatical reasons behind this is, unfortunately, way outside the scope of this book. At any rate, it's likely much easier to learn this through experience than by memorizing lists of arcane phonological rules. But, if you're a glutton for punishment, a trip down the Wikipedia rabbit hole on Japanese phonology might be an interesting way to ~~waste~~ spend a weekend.

2

KANJI

The ancient Japanese originally had no writing system with which to record their spoken language. Eventually, they adopted (and adapted) the Chinese writing system to fill this need. Although no one is certain exactly when they were created, the characters used today in China (漢字 *hànzì*), Korea (한자 *hanja* – only used occasionally these days), and Japan (漢字 *kanji*) are thought to have originated several thousand years ago. From China, it is believed they made their way to the island nation of Japan via Korea. The word 漢字 *kanji* itself means "Han [i.e., Han Dynasty] Character."

In many cases, the Japanese borrowed characters that represented the meaning of an existing Japanese concept and assigned it a Japanese pronunciation. Other times, they used characters that just happened to sound similar to a Japanese word, regardless of the character's actual meaning. Although it's possible for someone who reads Japanese to also understand some written Chinese, the Chinese language has significantly more characters. And even the ones that look the same may not share the same meaning.

≈

Classifications

Kanji can be seen as belonging to 6 different categories called 六書 *rokusho*: pictographs, simple ideographs, compound ideographs, phonetic-ideographic characters, derivative characters, and phonetic loan characters.

Pictographs

象形文字 *shōkei moji* [image-shape-character]

Many kanji started out as stylized pictures of the things they were describing. Examples of this type of character are 日 (sun), 月 (moon), 木 (wood/tree), 目 (eye), 耳 (ear), 山 (mountain), and 川 (river).

Simple Ideographs

指事文字 *shiji moji* [point-(to)-thing-character]

This type of kanji represents an abstract concept or object. Examples include 上 *ue* (up), 下 *shita* (down), and 中 *naka* (middle).

Phonetic-Ideographic Characters

形声文字 *keisei moji* [shape-voice-character]

These characters are a combination of one element representing an object with another element being used for phonetics, or pronunciation. Over 90% of all characters belong to this category.

氵 (water) + 可 (can/possible) = 河 (river)

人 (person) + 寺 (temple) = 侍 (samurai)

手 (hand) + 寺 (temple) = 持 (hold/grasp)

Note: Even the character for 寺 temple itself can be further broken down into 土 (earth/soil) and 寸 (measure).

Compound Ideographs

会意文字 *kaii moji* [meet-meaning-character]

This type of character combines existing simple ideographs to create new kanji based on a combined meaning of the component characters. Here are some examples:

日 (sun) + 月 (moon) = 明 (bright)

日 (sun) + 門 (gate) = 間 (interval/space)

Derivative Characters

転注文字 *tenchū moji* [change-note-character]

These kanji use a variation on the original meaning of a character, indicating something similar or related to the original meaning. For example, because 楽 *gaku* (music) is enjoyable, the character also came to mean "enjoyable."

Phonetic Loan Characters

仮借文字 *kashaku moji* [temporary-borrow-character]

These characters are chosen for their pronunciation, with little or no regard for their original meaning. While modern Japanese generally tends to use katakana to render foreign names and words, occasionally the names of countries and major cities are written with these characters. 亜米利加 *amerika* (America) and 亜細亜 *Ajia* (Asia) are examples of characters selected solely for their pronunciation.

Radicals: The Building Blocks of Kanji

Many of the more complex kanji are, in reality, not actually all that complex, but are rather made up of pieces that have their own meanings and which are repeatedly used in other characters. These parts, known as 部首 *bushu* [part-neck] or *radicals*, help to classify the kanji into groups and can be used as an index of sorts when looking up unfamiliar kanji. These radicals can, with some study, become easily identifiable, enabling one to recognize some of the complex kanji more easily.

Following is a list of the 214 traditional radicals used in Japanese kanji:

一中丶ノ乙亅二亠人儿入八冂冖冫几凵刀力勹匕匚匸十卜卩厂厶又口囗
土士夊夂夕大女子宀寸小尢尸屮山川工己巾干幺广廴廾弋弓彐彡彳心戈
戸手攴攵文斗斤方无日曰月木欠止歹殳毋比毛氏气水火爪父爻爿片牙牛
犬玄玉瓜瓦甘生用田疋疒癶白皮皿目矛矢石示禸禾穴立竹米糸缶网羊羽
老而耒耳聿肉臣自至臼舌舛舟艮色艸虍虫血行衣西見角言谷豆豕豸貝赤
走足身車辛辰辵邑酉釆里金長門阜隷隹雨青非面革韋韭音頁風飛食首香
馬骨高髟鬥鬯鬲鬼魚鳥鹵鹿麥麻黄黍黒黹黽鼎鼓鼠鼻齊齒龍龜龠

Obviously, an exhaustive treatise on the subject of radicals could quickly get out of hand. Instead, I will focus on only some of the most basic radicals that the average Aikidō student is likely to run into.

The Most Common Radicals

As of 2010, there are 2,136 characters that are considered 常用漢字 *jōyō kanji* or common-use characters. Perhaps surprisingly, only 6 radicals (with 略体 *ryakutai* abbreviated forms, shown in square brackets) are needed to help you recognize nearly 25% of these common characters, many of which fit into the *pictograph* category.

口 mouth

水 [氵] water

木 tree

人 [亻] person

手 [扌] hand

心 [忄 · 小] heart

If you add 12 more radicals, the number of kanji you can recognize climbs to 50%.

言 word

日 sun or day

糸 [纟] thread

肉 [月] meat / moon

土 ground

辶 road

艹 plant

宀 crown

貝 shell

女 woman

阝 wall (on left) / village (on right)

金 gold or metal

Finally, if you add another 30 radicals to the above, you've got about 75% covered.

一 one

刀 [刂] sword

十 ten

田 rice field

火 [灬] fire

大 big

山 mountain

食 meal

車 vehicle

彳 to go

目 eye

雨 rain

犬 dog

玉・王 ball・king

石 stone

力 power

衣 [衤] garment

弓 bow (weapon)

竹 [⺮] bamboo

又 again

攵 whip

示/⺬ display on an altar

酉 rooster [*alcohol* radical]

囗 enclosure

禾 grain

厂 cliff

疒 sickness

巾 (きん/はば) cloth

尸 (し) corpse

寸 inch/degree

As you can see, learning only 48 radicals will allow you *some* degree of recognition of over 1,600 kanji. However, this doesn't mean you will necessarily have a deep understanding of them. For example, while you might recognize that a character represents some kind of tree, bird, or fish, you may not know that it's an oak, an eagle, or a salmon.

Of course, not all of Japanese characters are commonly used in Aikidō-related terminology. So, unless you want to learn to read and write Japanese in a larger context, you probably don't need to know 1,600 characters. But, if you're interested in really digging into kanji (and like big, thick books), I recommend you look for a copy of The Nelson Japanese-English Character Dictionary. The new edition is blue, but I prefer the older red-covered version. Of course, there are also mobile apps and websites that put pretty much the same information at your fingertips (often more easily and cheaply) but I'm a bit old-school and have an affinity for books.

Common Positions of Radicals

Radicals do not always show up in the same place in every character. They can appear on the left side, top, and in various other locations. Remember also that there are different forms of the radicals as shown previously in square brackets earlier. The root character that the radical is based upon will often change its appearance based on its position in the character (we'll look at those later). The following should give you a basic idea of what is possible vis-à-vis radicals.

When the radical appears in the left-hand side of the kanji, it is known as *hen* (偏), or "inclination, bias." Remember that the original character used in the radical will often change form when it is in this position.

人 person

侍 samurai = 亻(person) + 寺 (temple)

信 trust = 亻(person) + 言 (word)

手 hand

持 to grasp = 手 (hand) + 寺 (temple)

捕 to seize = 手 (hand) + 甫 (first time, not until)

水 water

酒 rice wine (*sake*) = 水 (water) + 西 (west)

浪 waves = 水 (water) + 良 (good)

A 浪人 *rōnin* (masterless samurai) is like a person riding the waves.

Many other characters can be used as *hen,* but to try to cover all of them here would basically require writing a dictionary.

When the radical is on the right hand of the kanji, it is known as *tsukuri* (旁), or "incidental."

立刀 standing sword

刊 publish; carve = 干 (dry) + 刀 (sword)

列 rank, row = 歹 (bare-bone) + 刀 (sword)

力 strength

功 achievement = 工 (craft) + 力 (strength)

助 help, assist = 目 (eye) + 力 (strength)

When the radical is on the top, it is known as *kanmuri* (冠), or "crown." (This is where the name Toyota *Camry* comes from.)

宀 "u"

家 house; family = 宀 (crown) + 豕 (pig)

安 safe = 宀 (crown) + 女 (woman)

雨 rain

雷 thunder = 雨 (rain) + 田 (rice paddy)

雪 snow = 雨 (rain) + ヨ (pig head)

When the radical appears on the bottom of the kanji, it is known as *ashi* (脚), or "leg." As with *hen* and *tsukuri*, the original form of the character will often be changed—sometimes radically—in this position.

心 heart

忍 persevere = 刃 (blade) + 心 (heart)

想 concept, idea = 木 (tree) + 目 (eye) + 心 (heart)

儿 legs

元 original = 二 (two) + 儿 (legs)

兄 elder brother = 口 (mouth) + 儿 (legs)

When the radical surrounds all or part of the kanji, it is known as *kamae* (構), or "posture." This particular radical can come in multiple flavors, surrounding 2, 3, or all 4 sides of a kanji.

囗 box

回 rotate = 囗 (box) + 口 (mouth)

国 country = 囗 (box) + 玉 (jewel)

Note: the older form of this character is more complex: 國

門 gate

間 interval = 門 (gate) + 日 (sun)

聞 to listen = 門 (gate) + 耳 (ear)

冂 display

内 inside = 冂 (display) + 人 (person)

円 circle; Yen (Japanese monetary unit)

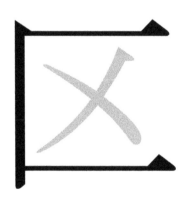

匚 enclose

医 medicine = 匚 (enclose) + 矢 (arrow)

区 district = 匚 (enclose) + 品 (goods)

Note: 区 is a simplified version of the older 區.

⺀ steam

氣 energy = ⺀ (steam) + 米 (rice)

Note: The character 気 ki is a simplified version of 氣.

When the radical surrounds the top and left portion of the kanji, it is known as *tare* (垂), or "hang."

厂 cliff

原 original = 厂 (cliff) + 白 (white) + 小 (small)

厄 bad luck = 厂 (cliff) + 卩 (seal)

ﾏ flag

尺 approx. 1 foot ﾏ (flag) + ヽ (dot)

居 to be, exist = ﾏ (flag) + 十 (ten) + 口 (mouth)

(The character 居 is used in the name of the art 居合道 *Iaidō*.)

When the radical surrounds the bottom and left portion of the kanji, it is known as 繞 *nyō*, or "surround, enclose."

辶 road

返 to turn/return = 辶 (road) + 厂 (cliff) + 又 (also)

道 road, path = 辶 (road) + 首 (neck)

You will recall that I mentioned earlier that when a character appears in different radical positions, the form of that character can change (hence, the alternative forms listed above), sometimes significantly. Here are a few examples to get you started:

火 fire

left side: 爆 to explode [火]

bottom: 熱 heat; fever [灬]

心 heart

left side: 情 feelings [忄]

bottom: 思 to think [心]

水 water

left side: 酒 alcohol [氵]

bottom: 泉 fountain [水]

~

Numbers

Finally, let's end with a discussion of numbers. Counting in Japanese is relatively easy... to a point. After 10,000, things are done a little differently than the Westerner may be accustomed to (e.g. 100,000 is 10 10,000). Fortunately, Aikidō students rarely have to count that high, so this shouldn't be a major problem.

1 一 壱 *ichi*

2 二 弐 *ni*

3 三 参 *san*

4 四 *shi/yon*

5 五 *go*

6 六 *roku*

7 七 *shichi*

8 八 *hachi*

9 九 *kū*

10 十 *jū*

You'll notice that there are two different characters listed for 1, 2, and 3. This is because the characters for these numbers are extremely easy to change, making the potential for counterfeiting a real concern. In order to fix this problem, deliberately-complex kanji are sometimes used on official documents, money, etc.

Although you won't likely need it, here's a basic idea of how to form numbers beyond 10. It's really quite logical and somewhat simple (even for 100,000 and above).

十一 11 *jūichi*

十二 12 *jūni*

二十 20 *nijū*

二十五 25 *nijūgo*

五十 50 *gojū*

百 100 *hyaku*

千 1,000 *sen*

一万 10,000 *ichiman*

十万 100,000 *jūman*

百万 1,000,000 *hyakuman*

Now that we have the preliminaries out of the way, let's dive into the kanji you're most likely to see during your study of Aikidō.

3

THE FAMILY TREE

植芝盛平 *Ueshiba Morihei* (aka 守高 *Moritaka* / 常盛 *Tsunemori*) was born on December 14, 1883 in 和歌山県 *Wakayama-ken* in a village that is now part of present-day 田辺市 *Tanabe-shi*. Since there are many in depth biographies of him in existence, I will instead focus specifically on his martial arts background. In addition to practicing 相撲 *Sumō* and 柔道 *Jūdō* in his youth, Ueshiba's name is also associated with the following arts and religions:

Daitō-ryū Aiki Jūjutsu
大東流合気柔術

武田惣角 *Takeda Sōkaku* was Ueshiba Morihei's Daitō-ryū teacher. Although Aikidō may be the most famous of Daitō-ryū's offspring, four major branches—with further sub-branches—of Daitō-ryū still exist today, each descending from one of these students of Takeda:

武田時宗 *Takeda Tokimune*, Sōkaku's son, taught 近藤勝之 *Kondō Katsuyuki*, the current headmaster of what is claimed to be the mainline of Daitō-ryū.

久琢磨 *Hisa Takuma* (his students formed the 琢磨会 *Takumakai*)

堀川幸道 *Horikawa Kōdō* (his students formed the 幸道会 *Kōdōkai*.) One well-known off-shoot of this group is 大東流合気柔術六方会 *Daitō-ryū Aikijūjutsu Roppōkai*, founded by 岡本正剛 *Okamoto Seigō*.

佐川幸義 *Sagawa Yukiyoshi*, considered to be the headmaster of Daitō-ryū during Tokimune's military service, was apparently notoriously secretive, especially when it came to non-Japanese. I, personally, am particularly bummed by this, as his dojo was a only a short drive from where I lived. Although I didn't know about him at the time, better-informed friends have since told me that, being a foreigner, I would've had no chance of gaining entrance to his dōjō anyway. *C'est la vie.*

Hapkido
合氣道 (합기도)

崔龍述 최용술 *Choi Yong-Sool*, founder of the Korean art Hapkido (the name of which, perhaps interestingly, is written with the same kanji as 合氣道 *Aikidō*) also claims to have been a direct student of Sōkaku. From my research, this assertion is a bit controversial, depending upon whom one talks to.

Note: I have met some early-generation students of Choi, and my own anecdotal opinion is that the art I saw them practicing did, indeed, seem *quite* similar to the Daitō-ryū I've seen. In fact, the flashy kicks often associated with Hapkido were completely absent from the version that I saw and even simple, low kicks appeared to be rare.

Early names for this art were 柔術 유술 *Yu Sool*, which is the Korean pronunciation of 柔術 *jūjutsu* and also 야와라 *Yawara*, an alternate name for jūjutsu derived from the native Japanese pronunciation of the first character in the name.

Also of interest is that Choi was, apparently, sometimes referred to in Korean by the title 道主 도주 *doju*, which uses the same kanji as *Dōshu* in Japanese, used to refer to the Chairman of the Aikikai Foundation.

Kitō-ryū Jūjutsu
起倒流柔術

A system of jūjutsu dating from the early Edo period. It is one of the systems studied by 嘉納治五郎 *Kanō Jigorō*, founder of Jūdō. Ueshiba Morihei studied both Kitō-ryū and Jūdō in his youth.

Tenjin Shinyō-ryū
天神真楊流

A school of jūjutsu dating from the late Edo period. It is another of the systems that Kanō Jigorō synthesized into what would be known as Kōdōkan Jūdō.

Yagyū Shingan-ryū
柳生心眼流

A classical Japanese martial art in which Ueshiba sensei received a mid-level license. 後藤派柳生流柔術 *Gotō-ha Yagyū-ryū Jūjutsu* is another name for this art.

~

Weapons Arts

Ueshiba likely derived his 合気杖 *aikijō* (aiki short staff) technique from a combination of 槍術 *sōjutsu* [spear-art] and 銃剣道 *jūkendō* [rifle-sword-way]. Ueshiba's aikijō appears to bear little resemblance to other systems of 杖術 *jōjutsu*, such as 神道夢想流 *Shintō Musō-ryū*. Ueshiba did, however, study other classical weapons systems.

Kashima Shin-ryū
鹿島神流

A classical Japanese 総合武術 *sōgō bujutsu* (comprehensive martial art) that features 剣術 *kenjutsu*, 抜刀術 *battojutsu*, 杖術 *jōjutsu*, 柔術 *jūjutsu*, 鎖鎌 *kusarigama*, and other arts.

Claims have been made that Ueshiba had studied Kashima Shin-ryū. However, according to Dr. Karl Friday, menkyo kaiden of Kashima Shin-ryū: "Ueshiba most definitely did not study Kashima Shin-ryū. Far from it, he and 国井善弥 *Kunii Zen'ya*, the Kashima Shin-ryū headmaster during Ueshiba's lifetime, were semi-friendly rivals, and Kunii was quite vocal (and public) in his criticism of Ueshiba's ideas about martial art."

Dr. Friday went on to say that "Ueshiba is, however, believed to have studied at least a bit of 直心影流 *Jikishin Kage-ryū* (apparently mostly under his Daitō-ryū master, *Takeda Sōkaku*, although the veracity of *Takeda*'s relationship to *Jikishin Kage-ryū* is uncertain). *Jikishin Kage-ryū* is more formally known as 鹿島神傳直心影流 *Kashima Shinden Jikishin Kage-ryū* ("direct reflections of the heart style, divinely transmitted from Kashima"), which may be where the source ... got confused. Both ryū-ha claim 上泉伊勢守 *Kamiizumi Ise-no-Kami* in their lineage, and are therefore related schools, but Kashima Shin-ryū is also heavily influenced by the (Kashima / Katori) Shintō-ryū tradition—the version thereof transmitted within the Kunii family. By Ueshiba's time, therefore, the two arts had become *very* different, even though they still share some common ideas and vocabulary." [Note: *I have edited all quotes to include certain kanji and translations. Any mistakes are my own.*]

Yagyu Shinkage-ryū
柳生新陰流

Ueshiba studied Yagyū Shinkage-ryū for about 5 years under 中井正勝 *Nakai Masakatsu*, the same man who taught and licensed him in Gotō-ha Yagyū Shingan-ryū.

∿

宗教 *shūkyō—Religions*

Ueshiba was arguably just as influenced by his religious/spiritual practices as he was by those in martial arts. Here is a look at a few major ones with which he was associated.

Shingon Buddhism
真言宗 *shingon shū*

A major school of 仏教 *bukkyō* Buddhism in Japan. Shingon means "true words," which is apparently a translation of the Sanskrit word मंत्र (mantra).

Shintō
神道

Originating in 古事記 *Kojiki* Records of Ancient Matters—Japan's oldest written historical record—Shintō is a native Japanese system of beliefs, mythologies, and ritual practices which teaches that the divine exists in all things (e.g., humans, rocks, trees, rivers, etc.). Shintō means "Divine Way" or "Way of the Gods." Many Aikidō dōjō have Shintō shrines.

Ōmoto-Kyō
大本教

Ōmoto-Kyō is a 神道 *Shintō* sect, founded by 出口王仁三郎 *Deguchi Onisaburō*, which heavily influenced Ueshiba Morihei's spiritual philosophy. It was Deguchi who purportedly deduced that Morihei's true purpose in life was to "teach the real meaning of Budō: an end to all fighting and contention." Deguchi was also responsible for leading Ueshiba to Mongolia in an attempt to establish a "utopian community." Ueshiba and others were imprisoned by the Chinese army for plotting an overthrow of the government (see the Aikidō chapter for more information regarding this). Ōmoto-Kyō means "Foundational Doctrine."

Ueshiba is known to have used various names for both his art and dōjō over the years. Among those names are the following examples:

Ueshiba-ha Daitō-ryū Aikibudō
植芝派大東流合気武道

An early name for Ueshiba's pre-Aikidō art. The 派 *ha* which follows Ueshiba's name means "faction" or "sect" and indicates his personal deviation from the 流 *ryū*, or "flow." This could be translated as Ueshiba-style or Ueshiba-faction.

Aikibudō
合気武道

Another early name for the art Ueshiba sensei taught after he started making changes to Daitō-ryū. Other systems of Aiki, such as 自由心流 合気武道 *Jiyūshin-ryū Aikibudō*, still use this name.

Ueshiba Juku
植芝塾

One of one of Ueshiba's early dōjō names. (A *juku* is a private school.)

Kōbukan Dōjō
皇武館道場

Another early Ueshiba dōjō. Affectionately known as "Hell Dōjō," the name more literally translates to "Imperial Military Hall Dojo."

Progeny

Aikikai Public Interest Incorporated Foundation
公益財団法人合気会 *kōeki zaidan hōjin aikikai*

Aikikai is an example of 家元 *iemoto* [family-foundation], a system in which leadership is hereditary. The Aikikai 本部道場 *Hombu Dōjō* [headquarters dōjō] is located in 東京都 *Tōkyō*.

International Aikido Federation
国際合気道連盟 *kokusai aikidō renmei*

The IAF is the international federation of Aikidō organizations which are directly affiliated with the Aikikai Hombu Dōjō in Japan. The President is always the current 道主 *dōshu*, or Chairman of the Aikikai Foundation. At the time of this writing, the current Dōshu is Ueshiba Moriteru, grandson of the Founder.

富木合気道
Tomiki Aikidō

Tomiki Aikidō was developed by 富木謙治 *Tomiki Kenji*, Waseda University professor and direct student of both Ueshiba Morihei and Kanō Jigorō. He was Aikidō's first 免許皆伝 *menkyo kaiden* and eventually held 8th dan in both Aikidō and Jūdō. Although primarily known for introducing the notion of competition into Aikidō, the Tomiki system is actually somewhat of a historical record of Ueshiba's Daitō-ryū period, with several 古流の形 *koryū-no-kata* [old-style kata] which preserve many older Daitō-ryū techniques that are conspicuously absent from much of the Aikidō practiced today.

In 2012, the Tomiki world split into two factions: 日本合気道協会 *Nihon Aikidō Kyōkai* Japan Aikidō Association (JAA) under 志々田文明 *Shishida Fumiaki* and the 昭道館合気道連盟 *Shōdōkan Aikido Renmei* Shōdōkan Aikido Federation (SAF) under 成山哲郎 Nariyama Tetsurō.

Yōshinkan Aikidō
養神館合気道

Founded by 塩田剛三 *Shioda Gōzō*, this style of Aikidō is headquartered at the 養神館 *Yōshinkan* in Tōkyō and is taught to members of the Tokyo Metropolitan Riot Police.

Yōseikan Budō
養正館武道

A comprehensive budo founded by 望月稔 *Mochizuki Minoru*, a high-ranking practitioner of 合気道 *Aikidō*, 柔道 *Jūdō*, 柔術 *Jūjutsu*, 空手 *Karate*, 古武道 *Kobudō*, 居合道 *Iaidō*, and 剣道 *Kendō*. Mochizuki was a direct student of 嘉納治五郎 *Kanō Jigorō* (Founder of Jūdō), 三船久蔵 *Mifune Kyūzō* (10ᵗʰ dan, nicknamed 柔道の神様 *Jūdō no Kami-sama*, or "The God of Jūdō"), 植芝盛平 *Ueshiba Morihei* (Founder of Aikidō), and 船越義珍 *Funakoshi Gichin* (Founder of Shotokan Karate).

Ki no Kenkyukai / Ki Society
氣の研究会

藤平光一 *Tōhei Kōichi*, former Chief Instructor of the Aikikai Hombu Dōjō, founded the Ki Society in 1971 after the death of Ueshiba but before his official departure from the Aikikai in 1974. Tōhei is famous for introducing Aikidō to the West, traveling to Hawai'i, the United States, and Europe starting in 1953.

While this style is sometimes called "Ki Aikidō" in the West, its Japanese name is 心身統一合気道 *Shinshin Tōitsu Aikidō*, or "Aikidō with Mind and Body Unified." Another name I heard often in Japan is 氣の研究会 *Ki no Kenkyūkai*, or the "Ki Research Organization." If you ever find yourself in 栃木県 *Tochigi-ken*, make sure to visit the 氣の博物館 *Ki no Hakubutsukan* (Ki Museum) near 氣の里 *Ki no Sato* (Ki Village).

Iwama Shinshin Aiki Shūrenkai
岩間神信合氣修練会

Often referred to as 岩間流 *Iwama-ryū* or Iwama Style. While the Iwama Dōjō was technically under the Aikikai during 斉藤守弘 *Saitō Morihiro's* lifetime, it was known for being stylistically distinct from other groups under the Aikikai umbrella. In 2002, two years after the death of his father, 斉藤仁弘 *Saitō Hitohiro*, broke from the Aikikai and created this organization to further the practice methods passed down to him. Since 2009, he has also gone by the name 仁平 *Hitohira*.

Aiki Manseidō
合氣万生道

Aikidō style and organization founded in 熊本市 *Kumamoto-shi* in 1954 by 砂泊誠秀 *Sunadomari Kanshū*. Aiki Manseidō was formerly known as 万生館合気道 *Manseikan Aikidō*. This style of Aikidō is especially ubiquitous in 九州 *Kyūshū*.

Tendō-ryū Aikidō
天道流合気道

Founded in 1969 by 清水健二 *Shimizu Kenji*, one of the last personal students of Ueshiba, shortly after the death of his teacher. Shimizu held 4th dan in Jūdō before beginning Aikidō in 1963. Tendō-ryū Aikidō is particularly popular in Europe, especially Germany.

4
AIKIDŌ

Before we start talking about the meaning of Aikidō, I'd like to clear up a prevalent misconception. Although it is commonly believed that Ueshiba made the decision to call his art Aikidō because of a spiritual awakening, this is not actually the case. In fact, the name change was not even Ueshiba's idea at all, but was rather forced on him in 1942 by the 大日本武徳会 *Dai Nippon Butokukai* via 平井稔 *Hirai Minoru*, whom Ueshiba had appointed Director of General Affairs for the 皇武館道場 *Kōbukan Dōjō*.

Aikidō is sometimes translated as "the way of harmony with the universe." In the spirit of full disclosure, I must admit that I'm not a particular fan of this interpretation. One reason for this is that neither "harmony" nor "the universe" appears in the word itself. Another is that this notion is quite different from the original meaning of Aiki. More on that later in this chapter.

(To be fair, however, depending on how one defines it, I will admit that there may a certain degree of "harmony" that can be inferred from the kanji 合 *ai*, which means to fit or to be appropriate. Being appropriate and fitting into a situation can certainly imply an air of "harmony.")

When speaking of "harmony" in Japanese, one will often see the character 和 *wa* peace/harmony (e.g. 平和 *heiwa* [even-peace], 調和 *chōwa* [tone-peace], and 和声 *wasei* [harmony-voice]). But 和 *wa* harmony and the harmony you may be thinking of might not be the same thing. In my experience, *wa* has less concern for the individual; it's all about the overall harmony of the group as a whole. There's a well-known saying in Japanese which I think illustrates the Japanese notion of *wa* pretty well: 出る杭は打たれる *deru kui wa utareru* - "the post that sticks up gets hammered down." (Note that は *ha* is pronounced *wa* in this case because it is serving as a grammatical particle that marks the topic.)

It certainly isn't entirely uncommon for people to reach a very personal—sometimes poetic—level of understanding of a subject after many years of training. I don't begrudge anyone his or her own personal epiphanies. I, myself, sometimes use poetry when teaching my more experienced students... but only after they've attained a certain degree of understanding. Before that, it can just end up muddying the waters.

A possible source for the "harmony with the universe" notion could be the word Aikidō being broken down into its component characters (合・気・道), translated individually into English, then reassembled. These characters, when viewed separately, could be said to mean "the way of fitting to energy," which, I suppose, isn't all that far off from "harmony with the universe," depending upon how one views such things.

In his book "Dueling with O-sensei," Ellis Amdur quotes Ueshiba Morihei (via Mutō Masao quoting 竹下勇海軍大将 Admiral *Takeshita Isamu*) as saying:

> "Aiki is a means of achieving harmony with another person so that you can make them do what you want."

Now, it is not my intention to suggest you throw out your definition of Aiki and blindly accept what I am about to present, but rather to give you some extra food for thought to perhaps enhance your own understanding. It is my contention that, rather than looking at Aikidō as ai-ki-dō, it may—perhaps—be useful to consider it instead as Aiki-dō [the Way of *Aiki*]. (Note that American martial arts pioneer and author Donn F. Draeger wrote it as "aiki-do" multiple times in the 1973 edition of his book "Classical Bujutsu." I don't think one should necessarily read too much into this, but it is interesting nonetheless.)

Aiki

Ueshiba Morihei is purported to have said: 合気は愛である *aiki wa ai de aru* or "Aiki is Love." Because the word "love" is also pronounced *ai*, this makes for a rather clever, somewhat profound play on words. This interpretation of *aiki* would certainly appear to jibe with Ueshiba's spiritual beliefs, at least after his reported epiphany.

In 武産合気 *Takemusu Aiki*, a collection of transcribed lectures, Ueshiba Morihei said the following about Aikidō (translated by the author):

合気道とは、宇宙の万世一系の理であります。

aikidō to wa, uchū no bansei ikkei no ri de arimasu.

Aikidō is the principle of the eternal continuation of the Universe.

合気道とは、天授の真理にして、武産の合気の妙用であります。

aikidō to wa, tenju no shinri ni shite, takemusu no aiki no myōyō de arimasu.

Aikidō is heaven-sent truth, the mysterious result of Takemusu Aiki.

合気道とは、天地人、和合の道とこうなるのであります。

aikidō to wa, tenchijin, wagō no michi to kō naru no de arimasu.

Aikidō is Heaven, Earth, and Man united on the Harmonious Path.

また合気道とは、万有の処理の道であります。

mata aikidō to wa, ban'yū no shori no michi de arimasu.

Aikidō is also the Way of taking care of all things.

合気道とは、言霊の妙用であり、宇宙みそぎの大道であります。

aikidō to wa, kotodama no myōyō de ari, uchū misogi no daidō de arimasu.

Aikido is the mysterious result of kotodama (the soul of language) and the great Way of universal purification.

この道を思惟する人々は、宇宙建国完成の経綸に奉仕しなければなら
ないことになっております。

*kono michi wo shii suru hitobito wa, uchū kenkoku kansei no keirin ni hōshi
shinakereba naranai koto ni natte orimasu.*

Those who deeply contemplate this path must serve to administer the founding of a Universal Nation.

From the Founder's mouth, to paper, to my eyes, through my brain, directly to your eyeballs. Ueshiba's own words clear everything up, right? Unless you're an erudite Shintō priest who is also adept at Aikidō and has studied the history of the art itself... perhaps not.

Ueshiba was renowned for making references to works like 古事記 *kojiki* (also, *furukotofumi*) Records of Ancient Matters, from which many Shintō practices were derived. When you're trying to read a book that talks of the deities 国之常立神 *Kuninotokotachi-no-Kami* and 天之御中主神 *Amenominakanushi-no-Kami* summoning the god 伊邪那 岐命 *Izanagi-no-Mikoto* and goddess 伊邪那美命 *Izanami-no-Mikoto* to create the first land (Japan, naturally) by wielding 天之瓊矛 *Ame-no-Nu-Hoko* The Heavenly-Jeweled Spear and crossing the 天浮橋 *ame no ukihashi* or Floating Heavenly Bridge, things can get quite difficult to comprehend, even for the modern well-researched Japanese speaker.

I've read many accounts where even his Japanese students had a very difficult time understanding his lectures, so don't feel bad.

Incidentally, the above *misogi*, which you may have heard in your studies, is a reference to the ritual purification carried out by the aforementioned Izanagi-no-Mikoto which resulted in the birth of such deities as 天照大御神 *Amaterasu-Ōmikami* (goddess of the sun and universe), 月読尊 *Tsukuyomi-no-Mikoto* (god of the moon), and 須佐之男 *Susa-no-Ō* (god of sea and storms), also known as 建速須佐之男命 *Takehaya Susa-no-Ō-no-Mikoto*.

The "founding of a Universal Nation" Ueshiba talks about may have been a reference to the creation of a Utopia on Earth. In fact, he and his cohorts (including members of the 黑龍會 *Kokuryūkai* Black Dragon Society, a prominent right-wing ultranationalist paramilitary group of the time which had carried out espionage and assassinations for the Imperial Army during the Russo-Japanese war) were trying to create a Utopia in Mongolia in 1924 when they were arrested by Chinese authorities. Fortunately for Ueshiba, unlike his non-Japanese counterparts, he escaped the firing squad and was later released to the custody of the Japanese consulate.

> Q. Do I really need to understand all of this religion, language, and history to learn Aikidō?
>
> A. In my opinion, *absolutely not*. I happen to find some of it interesting, but it will never replace drenching the tatami with sweat and tears.

Let's get back to the topic at hand. We've seen that Ueshiba had some pretty mystical and religious definitions for aiki and Aikidō. But the word *aiki* preexists Ueshiba. This brings me to a new question: Is it possible that Ueshiba actually *changed* the definition of the already extant word *aiki* to fit his own spiritual purposes?

In "Daito-ryu Aikijujutsu: Conversations with Daito-ryu Masters" by Stan Pranin, Takeda Tokimune (Sōkaku's son) defined aiki thus:

"*Aiki* is to pull when you are pushed, and to push when you are pulled. It is the spirit of slowness and speed, of harmonizing your movement with your opponent's *ki*. Its opposite, *kiai*, is to push the limit, while *aiki* never resists."

Certainly, as we shall see, Ueshiba's use of the word differs from earlier uses in classical bujutsu. In an effort to explore this further, I have asked several high-level practitioners of various arts outside of mainstream Aikidō to share their understandings of the original meaning(s) of the concept.

C. E. Clark
Founder, Jiyūshin-ryū Aikibudō

The simple, and profound, meaning of aiki is very similar to yoga (i.e. to "yoke" something, or connect, join together). Aiki means *a harmonious joining of the spirit/energies*. The inherent values range from peaceful to violent depending on the situation. My personal motive is to always do the least amount of harm possible to reach the conclusion that is necessary to resolve the situation.

Tobin Threadgill
Kaicho, Takamura-ha Shindō Yōshin-ryū

We don't even use the term "aiki" in Takamura-ha Shindō Yōshin-ryū. Aiki originally came from swordsmanship, and in that context, it meant something akin to mental manipulation. If I can manipulate my adversary into involuntarily doing what I want him to do, it's easier to kill him. So if I can force him into harmonizing with my intent, he becomes one with me mentally. He is then no threat to me. Ueshiba was a mystic who redefined the term based on a Shintō concept of universal pacifism and harmony. Any time someone starts trying to define "Aiki," it's a flawed enterprise unless you strictly define parameters. Whatever name it goes by, aiki, 妙伝 *myōden*, whatever… it's out there in many guises.

Ellis Amdur
Toda-ha Bukō-ryū and Araki-ryū Torite Kogusoku

戸田派武甲流の合気 *Aiki* in *Toda-ha Bukō-ryū*

As is surely common knowledge, aiki is a word of vague and multifarious meaning. Not only is it defined differently among various martial systems, but even within a single martial art, different meanings are attributed to this phrase. Here, I will discuss what is, as far as I know, the oldest usage of the word within any extant martial system, that of the Toda-ha Bukō-ryū.

This martial tradition has its roots in the Chujō-ryū, often considered one of the three root martial systems from which most other ryū-ha emanated. The Chujō-ryū begot the Toda-ryū, and among the offshoots of this school was a family martial system associated with the Suneya family located deep in a mountainous area in present-day Saitama prefecture, called Chichibu. In the mid-1800's, Suneya Ryōsuke and his wife reworked the Suneya family martial art into Toda-ha Bukō-ryū. This system emphasizes the study of the 薙刀 *naginata* (glaive), in particular the 鍵付薙刀 *kagitsuki-naginata*, a glaive with a cross-bar, which was used to pin or break an enemy's blade.

A very important subsidiary weapon in this school is the 鎖鎌 *kusarigama* (chain-and-sickle). There are two sets of five kata that feature this weapon: one set is rather typical, featuring the kusarigama in the *shitachi* (the *nage/tori* in Aikidō) and sword in the *uketachi* (*uke* in Aikidō) role. The other set, however, is rather remarkable, featuring the naginata in the shitachi role and kusarigama in the uketachi. I am aware of no other ryū with any similar kata set. This set is called 鎌鎌 合気之事 (*Kusarigama Aiki no Koto*).

This set of kata is located in the *chūden* (middle) level of training. In this intermediate level, one is assumed to have become well-versed in the basics of the school. Here, the use of the kusarigama against the central weapon of the school, the naginata, one is introduced a number of very important parameters in training. First of all is variable *ma'ai*. The metal weight on a kusarigama can injure or even kill, and depending upon how it is used, it often can reach up to a meter further than shidachi expects. Thus, these *kata* teach the naginata fighter how to evaluate angle of attack, combative spacing, and speed of a flying object.

Another very important point is revealed in the use of the word, 合気 *aiki*, within the name of this set. This word can bear a variety of meanings: particularly notable is the use of the term, meaning "internal power" or "integrated, whole body force" in such ryū-ha as Kitō-ryū and Daitō-ryū Jūjutsu. The word is used in much more prosaic fashion here, meaning "fitting together." Four of the five kata in this set end in with the naginata fighter cutting 正面切り *shomengiri* [cut to the front], to be received with the top of the kusarigama, a combatively absurd block that puts uketachi at physical risk. What these kata require is that shidachi cuts with perfect precision: not too powerfully, but at the same time absolutely straight, so that uketachi (who is either senior or *sensei*) is not injured. This puts shidachi under a remarkable psychological stress—particularly considering the cultural context when these kata were created.

In addition, it is absolutely essential that the naginata fighter learns to cut with such accuracy one can easily bend or break the blade of the naginata, or break the tang out of the shaft if one cuts at the wrong angle.

Lest there be any confusion, the naginata is a much more powerful weapon than the kusarigama, and a skilled practitioner can easily defeat a skilled kusarigama fighter (a weapon that is really suited to fight against a sword). Nonetheless, the kusarigama is a wonderful tool to teach *tai sabaki*, *ma'ai*, and for those who are not used to fast dangerous objects suddenly flying at one's head with lethal intent, courage.

Howard Popkin
Daitoryu Aikijujitsu Ginjukai

"Aiki" is, within the Japanese Budō community, the source of more division than the unity its kanji would profess. While the dictionary would say *ai* is harmony and *ki* energy, even amongst longtime practitioners, the mere discussion of aiki causes arguments.

Publicly, Okamoto Seigō sensei, Soshi of the Daitō-ryū Aikijūjutsu Roppōkai, explained that aiki is "breathing, circular movements, timing, and softness." In private, however, his definition was very different. He spoke of aiki as the "feeling and thinking of attack." Once, I asked him what he was thinking about; he said, "*Gomen nasai, Hawādo-san.*" (I'm sorry, Howard-san.) When I asked why he was apologizing, he replied, "I am thinking about putting a long spear about 4 feet through your head." He didn't mean that in a *mean* way; he was simply describing the thought process he used to engage his intent to create "aiki."

Now that we've seen a bit about how people from systems outside the Aikidō orthodoxy understand *aiki*, let's dig into the constituent characters of the word itself: 合 *ai*, 気 *ki*, and 道 *dō*, with 武 *bu* thrown in for good measure.

合 *ai*—to fit; to be appropriate

This character is often seen in cases where fitting, appropriateness, and suitability are concerned. For example, 合わせ *awase* means "to fit together." In Aikidō terms, *awase* generally means fitting together in such a way that neither side has an advantage. Here are some more examples that use this character:

場合 *ba'ai* [location-fit] circumstance, situation

間合 *ma'ai* [interval-fit] refers to the distance between things. In Aikidō, the distance between you and your partner is called *ma'ai*. There are 3 basic levels of *ma'ai*:

- 遠い間合い *to'oi ma'ai* far distance
- 近間合い *chika ma'ai* close distance
- 内間合い *uchi ma'ai* inside distance

氣 / 気 *ki*—spirit; energy

Ahhh... the infamous *ki* (or *qi/chi* in Chinese). I could probably devote an entire chapter to this character alone. (Don't worry, I won't.) Note that there are two forms for this character used in Japanese: 氣 and 気. The first is an older form, while the latter is a simplified version. Looking at the original character, we can clearly see the radical 气 (spirit) escaping from 米 (rice). If you squint hard enough, you can almost see how "energy" might be derived from this character.

Rather than spark a *Ki War* over what ki is or isn't—or whether it even exists as a measurable physical phenomenon—I will instead endeavor to take a look at how this character is used elsewhere in colloquial Japanese. Hopefully, this will help you to develop a feel for the many, quite mundanely normal, ways in which this character is understood and used in Japan.

電気 *denki* [lightning-energy] means "electricity." Did you notice the radical for lightning is 雨 (rain)? The character almost looks like someone is flying a kite in a rainstorm. (This explanation doesn't actually hold any linguistic water, but it sure makes for a useful visual mnemonic.)

If someone asks if you're 元気 *genki* [original-spirit] they're not exactly asking "how are you?" but whether you are in "original spirits." The appropriate response is はい *hai* (yes) or いいえ *iie* (no) along with other words thanking them for their role in your genki-ness, such as 御陰さまで *okagesama de* or "thanks to you (the *other side*)."

Following what we've discussed so far regarding ki, it seems almost natural to interpret the various meteorological phenomena as reflections of the "spirit of heaven." As such, 天気 *tenki* [heaven-spirit] means "weather."

If you are 病気 *byōki* [sick-spirit], you are ill. If your spirit were sick, it might make sense that your body would be sick as well.

気合 *kiai* [spirit-appropriate/fit] describes fighting spirit or willpower. In some instances, it can be a spirited shout. 気合 is the "reverse" of 合気, and is often found in such phrases as 気合いがない *kiai ga nai* "to have no willpower" (lit: "to have no kiai") and 気合いを入れる *kiai wo ireru* "to psych one's self up" (lit: "to insert kiai"). Contrary to what some English-speaking martial arts world might think, 気合 does not necessarily require one to shout, nor should one actually yell the word "KIAI!" (Or, "KIHAP!" as I've heard from some in the Korean arts.)

道 dō—path, road, way

Also pronounced *michi*, 道 (*dào* in Chinese) is a character steeped in centuries of writings in both Japan and China. The Daoist classic 道德經 *Dao De Jing/Tao Te Ching*—or 道徳経 *Dōtokukyō* "Virtuous Sutra of The Way" as it is written in modern Japanese—declares that *The Way* is something that cannot be spoken of.

道可道，非常道。 *dào kě dào, fēi cháng dào.*

名可名，非常名。 *míng kě míng, fēi cháng míng.*

Dao can be talked about, but not the Eternal Dao.

Names can be named, but not the Eternal Name.

So... let's talk about it.

The 道場 *dōjō* [path-place] is where you study the Way (in this case, Aiki-dō, the Way of Aiki). A 国道 *kokudō* [national-path] is what we might call an interstate highway in The United States. The character 道 also finds its way into the names of several traditional Japanese arts, including 茶道 *chadō/sadō* [tea-way] Tea Ceremony, 柔道 *jūdō* [flexible-way] Jūdō, 書道 *shodō* [writing-way] Japanese calligraphy, and 空手道 *karatedō* [empty-hand-way] Karate-dō. Note that Karate was originally written 唐手道 *karatedō* [Tang-hand-way]), but once it was introduced to the mainland from 沖縄 *Okinawa*, the Japanese changed the character 唐 *kara* (Tang dynasty China) into 空 *kara* (empty). Interestingly, the Korean art of 당수도 *Tang Soo Do* is still written 唐手道 when hanja is used.

Some teachers, including Ueshiba Morihei, even write songs or poems to pass on knowledge or philosophy that would otherwise be difficult to express. These are called 道歌 *dōka* or "song of the way." More on them in a later chapter.

武 *bu*—martial, military

The character 武 shows up in a number of places, including 武道 *budō* [martial-way] budō, 武術 *bujutsu* [martial-science] bujutsu, 武士 *bushi* [martial-gentleman] warrior, 武士道 *bushidō* [martial-gentleman-way] Bushidō, 日本武道館 *Nippon Budōkan* Japan Martial Arts Hall (located in Tōkyō), and 大日本武徳会 *Dai-Nippon Butokukai* [Great-Japan-Martial-Virtue-Society].

An oft-told story purports that this character is composed of the kanji 戈 (halberd) and 止 (to stop), suggesting that 武 means "to stop the halberd" or to put an end to warfare. Allegedly, this comes from a Confucian writing: 戈を止めるを武と為す *hoko wo tomeru wo bu to nasu* (to stop the halberd results in *bu*). This is, however, generally considered to be an incorrect interpretation, and the character is more likely to mean "to advance with the spear." It is very easy to arbitrarily assign incorrect meanings to kanji to suit ones own needs or beliefs. It is this very fact which caused me to undertake the laborious journey of researching and writing this book in the first place.

Now that we have an idea (or two) of what the name Aikidō might mean, we're ready to take the first steps along the path. If you have 初心 *shoshin* [begin-heart], you have "beginner's mind." A beginner is called 初心者 *shoshinsha* [begin-heart-person]. So, let's begin at the beginning.

5

RANKS

段級位制

The Ranking System

The 段級位制 *dan-kyū isei* ranking system used in 現代武道 *gendai budō* [modern martial ways] traces its beginnings to the ancient game of 囲碁 *i-Go* (often referred to simply as *Go*). Go, thought to be over 2,500 years old, is a strategic board game in which two players—using white and black stones—attempt to capture territory. Perhaps interestingly, the video game company Atari gets its name from Go. 当たり *atari*, the nominal form of the intransitive verb 当たる *ataru* (to strike or contact a target, or to receive something fortuitously) means something similar to "check" in a game of chess. Also interesting—and more relevant to the subject of this book—is that the word 当身 *atemi* [strike/contact-body] (discussed in Attacks) comes from the transitive form (当てる *ateru*) of this same verb.

嘉納治五郎 *Kanō Jigorō* was the first to apply this ranking system to 柔道 *jūdō* in 1883. Think about that year for a moment. As famous as the idea of the "black belt" is today, it has only existed for a little over a century. Before that, there were no "black belts" in Japanese martial arts. Since Kanō's adoption, however, it has come to be almost universally used in Asian martial arts.

Just as—as mentioned earlier—the 大日本武徳会 *Dai Nippon Butokukai* forced Ueshiba to rename his art to Aikidō, so too did they require him to start using the dan-kyū system in order to bring Aikidō into line with other gendai budō throughout Japan. However, multiple accounts suggest that Ueshiba didn't take this very seriously and regularly promoted people to whatever rank suited the whim of the day, even promoting people to 9th and 10th dan because he thought they had achieved a glimpse of understanding.

The dan-kyū system of today comprises two levels—mudansha and yudansha—with multiple levels within both dan and kyū.

Mudansha

In the 段級 *dan-kyū* ranking system, anyone under the rank of black belt is generally considered a 無段者 *mudansha* [no-grade-person]. Unfortunately, no uniform grading system for the mudansha ranks exists between the various traditions of Aikidō, nor does every school use all 10 kyū levels. The ungraded ranks are (with 1st being the highest):

10th *kyū* 十級 *jūkyū*

9th *kyū* 九級 *kyūkyū*

8th *kyū* 八級 *hachikyū*

7th *kyū* 七級 *nanakyū*

6th *kyū* 六級 *rokkyū*

5th *kyū* 五級 *gokyū*

4th *kyū* 四級 *yonkyū*

3rd *kyū* 三級 *sankyū*

2nd *kyū* 二級 *nikyū*

1st *kyū* 一級 *ikkyū*

Yūdansha

A practitioner who has achieved 1st degree black belt (or higher) is known as a 有段者 *yūdansha* [have-grade-person]. In general, mainstream Aikidō uses only black belt for yūdansha ranks, but some systems incorporate other colors. This will be discussed more in the Equipment chapter in the section on clothing.

1st *dan* 初段 *shōdan* [beginning-step]

2nd *dan* 二段 / 弐段 *nidan*

3rd *dan* 三段 / 参段 *sandan*

4th *dan* 四段 *yodan/yondan*

5th *dan* 五段 *godan*

6th *dan* 六段 *rokudan*

7th *dan* 七段 *nanadan*

8th *dan* 八段 *hachidan*

9th *dan* 九段 *kudan/kyūdan*

10th *dan* 十段 *jūdan*

Note that 1st degree black belt is not called "1st" *dan* in Japanese, but "beginning" *dan*. I think that's pretty significant. Another point hearkens back to how the numbers from 1-3 were made more complex to foil attempts at counterfeiting. As such, nidan can be written both 二段 and 弐段, and sandan can be written both 三段 and 参段. Finally, a high-ranking blackbelt is sometimes referred to as a 高段者 *kōdansha* [high-dan-person].

Juniors and Seniors

後輩 *kōhai* [after-comrade] junior

先輩 *sempai* [before-comrade] senior

Students

There are various terms for students in Japanese, from the more generic terms 生徒 *seito* [live-junior], 学生 *gakusei* [study-live] secondary education student, and 大学生 *daigakusei* [big-study-live] college student to the more disciple-esque 門下生 *monkasei* [gate-below-live]. A close apprentice of a teacher can be called a 弟子 *deshi* [younger brother-child]. A student living in the dōjō and training regularly under their teacher's watchful eye can be called an 内弟子 *uchideshi* [inside-apprentice], while one who lives outside the dōjō would be called a 外弟子 *sotodeshi* [outside-apprentice]. I have heard some people (non Japanese speakers), on rare occasion, claim that uchideshi means "in-house student," suggesting that they perhaps think the *uchi* portion of the word is 家 *uchi*, or house.

Someone who travels with their teacher—often taking care of their teacher, carrying his or her bags, assisting as demo uke, and helping out by performing miscellaneous tasks—is often called お供 *otomo*, which means attendant or companion.

Finally, someone who engages in Aikidō—teachers and students alike—can refer to him or herself as 合気道家 *aikidōka* [Aikidō practitioner]. However, in my experience, there is an air of longevity and seriousness implied by this appellation. I, personally, didn't start thinking of myself as a Budōka until *long* after I became a yūdansha.

Teachers

The most common term of address for any sort of teacher in Japanese is 先生 *sensei* [before-live]. If said teacher is a college professor, you might see them referred to as 教授 *kyōju* [teach-confer] or 博士 *hakase* [Doctor/PhD] in writing, but the term of address is still *sensei*. Let's look at some Aikidō-specific words for teachers.

Ueshiba Morihei is often referred to as "O-Sensei." (Not to be confused with his Irish cousin, O'Sensei.) He isn't alone. If you mention "O-Sensei" in conversation with people from different martial arts, you may be asked "which one?" Students of other arts have their own highly respected teachers, and they may not even know of Ueshiba sensei.

Although 大先生 *ōsensei* [great-teacher] (also read *daisensei*) has come into common use, especially in the English-speaking world, it seems to me that that 翁先生 *ōsensei*, or "venerable old teacher," is perhaps more commonly used in Japanese-language Aikidō literature. In fact, Ueshiba sensei used to refer to himself as 盛平翁 *Morihei-ō* or "Venerable Old Man Morihei."

To research this a little more, I used a quick-and-dirty linguist trick: I did a corpus search using Google Japan. Here are my results (which will have undoubtedly changed by the time you read this):

大先生: 1,080,000 hits

翁先生: 544,000 hits

While those numbers might suggest that the word 大先生 is more common in Japanese, when I searched for 翁先生, the first result that popped up on Google Japan was the Japanese Wikipedia entry for Ueshiba sensei. In contrast, a search for 大先生 didn't even produce his name until page 10. While such impromptu research certainly isn't conclusive from a linguistic standpoint, it is nonetheless interesting.

Another form of reference I have heard original students (e.g. Saitō Morihiro) of Ueshiba sensei use is 開祖 *kaisō* [open-ancestor], or "Founder."

While I suppose it could be *technically* correct to refer to Ueshiba Morihei as 宗家 *sōke* [origin-family] in some sense, he is more often referred to as the first 道主 *dōshu* [way-master] or Chairman of the Aikikai Foundation. As of this printing, there have been 3 Aikikai Dōshu:

初代道主 *shodai* [1st generation] *dōshu* 植芝盛平 Ueshiba Morihei

二代道主 *nidai* [2nd generation] *dōshu* 植芝吉祥丸 Ueshiba Kisshōmaru

三代道主 *sandai* [3rd generation] *dōshu* 植芝守央 Ueshiba Moriteru

The fourth generation Dōshu will likely be 植芝充央 *Ueshiba Mitsuteru*, son of Moriteru. Until he assumes that position, however, he may be referred to by another moniker. Occasionally, a young apprentice teacher who is being groomed to succeed his father/teacher will be called 若先生 *waka sensei* or "young teacher." Ueshiba Moriteru, himself, was referred to as such until his age made this inappropriate.

One often hears 養神館 *Yōshinkan* founder 塩田剛三 *Shioda Gōzō* referred to as 館長 *kanchō* [hall-chief], but technically, anyone who is in charge of a large dōjō could be called by the same name. Another term for the head of a dōjō is 道場長 *dōjō-chō* [way-place-chief]. The head of an organization can be called 会長 *kaichō*.

Levels of Teacher

Aikikai recognizes three levels of teaching license:

副指導員 *fukushidōin* [vice-shidōin] 2nd - 3rd dan

指導員 *shidōin* [point-guide-member] 4th - 5th dan

師範 *shihan* [expert-example] 6th dan & up

Some systems express levels of experience in other ways:

初伝 *shoden* [begin-transmission] beginning level

中伝 *chūden* [middle-transmission] mid-level

奥伝 *okuden* [interior-transmission] deep secrets

秘伝 *hiden* [secret-transmission] esoteric secrets

極意 *gokui* [highest-idea] the innermost secrets

The following senior-level titles are common to Japanese martial arts, but may not be used by your particular school:

錬士 *renshi* [refining-gentleman] 5th dan

教士 *kyōshi* [teacher-gentleman] 6th dan

範士 *hanshi* [model-gentleman] 7th dan

While it isn't readily apparent by looking at the Romanized versions of the words, a look at the kanji will quickly show you that 師範 *shihan* is not simply the reverse of 範士 *hanshi*. This is but one example of why a basic knowledge of kanji can prove useful and why I thought it a good idea to write this book in the first place.

Certificates and Licenses

In 1922, Ueshiba Morihei received the 教授代理 *kyōju dairi* [teach-impart-substitute-arrangement] license in Daitō-ryū Aikijūjutsu from his teacher Takeda Sōkaku. This license authorized Ueshiba to teach in Takeda's stead. The word 教授 *kyōju* means "professor" and 代理 *dairi* means "proxy" or "representative."

Daitō-ryū Certifications

秘伝目録 *hiden mokuroku* [secret-transmission-catalog] The base level of certification in Daitō-ryū which comprises 118 techniques. It contains 一ケ条 *ikkajō* (30 techniques), 二ケ条 *nikajō* (30 techniques),

三ヶ条 *sankajō* (30 techniques), 四ヶ条 *yonkajō* (15 techniques), 五ヶ条 *gokajō* (13 techniques)

合気之術 *aiki no jutsu* [aiki-art] (53 techniques)

秘伝奥義 *hiden ōgi* [secret-transmit-interior-meaning] (36 techniques) Secret Mysteries

護身用の手 *gōshin'yō no te* [defend-body-usage-hand] (84 techniques) Self Defense Techniques

解釈総伝 *kaishaku sōden* [understand-explain-full-transmission] (477 techniques) Explanation of Full Transmission

免許皆伝 *menkyo kaiden* [license-full-transmission] (88 techniques) License of Complete Transmission

Despite menkyo kaiden appearing to be more the purview of 古流武術 *kōryū būjutsu* old-style martial arts, it was actually used by Ueshiba in the early days. As mentioned earlier, the first person to receive this rank in Aikidō was Tomiki Kenji. When Aikidō switched over to the dan-kyu ranking system, Ueshiba decided that the equivalent of Tomiki's menkyo kaiden would be 8th dan.

Note: It may be of some tangential interest that the word 運転免許 *unten menkyo* means "driver's license." Just as an unten menkyo gives one license to drive a motor vehicle, menkyo kaiden gives one full license to teach a system.

免状の翻訳 *menjō no hon'yaku*—Certificate/License Translation

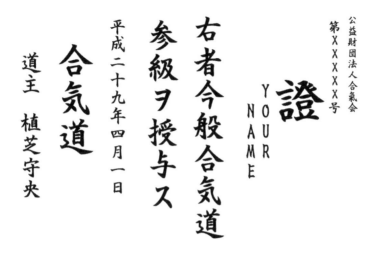

Sample Aikikai Rank Certificate — yours may look different

Chances are, if you've been training long enough, you've probably been through a 審査 *shinsa* promotion exam of some sort and may even have been promoted. Once promoted, you may have received a 證 *shō* (certificate) or 免状 *menjō* (license) of some sort. If the certificate is written in Japanese, chances also are that you may have little idea what it actually says. Let's attempt to remedy that right now. Note that this is modeled on an Aikikai certificate; different systems produce documents that can look very different and will use different language. But perhaps some of this will help you.

From top-to-bottom, right-to-left, it reads:

公益財団法人合気会 *kōeki zaidan hōjin aikikai*

Aikikai Public Interest Incorporated Foundation

第一二三四五六号 *dai ichi ni san shi go roku gō*

 # 123456

證 *shō* certificate; proof

(Your Name)

右者今般合気道 *migi no mono kon pan*

参級ヲ授与ス *aikidō 3-kyū wo juyo su*

To the person on the right is thus conferred the grade of 3rd kyū in Aikidō

平成二十九年四月一日 *heisei nijūkyū nen shigatsu tsuitachi*

Heisei 29 (2017) April 1st

合気道 *Aikidō*

道主 植芝守央 *Dōshu Ueshiba Moriteru*

6

COURTESY

武道は礼に始まり礼に終わる
budō wa rei ni hajimari rei ni owaru
Budō begins and ends with courtesy

Ueshiba Morihei was adamant that *Aikidō* is *Budō*. As such, it follows that Aikidō must also begin and end with courtesy. As an expression of this, we often use two phrases over and over in our training:

お願いします *onegai shimasu*

Onegai shimasu means something akin to "I have a favor to ask of you" or "please give me _____." This is what we say when asking someone to train with us. You may also hear something extra at the beginning: 宜しく *yoroshiku*, which can mean "best regards" or "well."

有り難うございます *arigatō gozaimasu*

Arigatō gozaimasu means "thank you." Unlike English, which uses "thank you" in the past, present, and future tenses, if you're thanking someone for something that has already happened (e.g. having just trained with you) in Japanese, past tense is used: *arigatō gozaimashita*. You may also hear the word *dōmo* before the above phrase, which means "very much."

五徳 Five Confucian Virtues

No conversation about Japanese customs would be complete without having a look at the five Confucian virtues, or 五徳 *gotoku*.

仁 *jin*—Benevolence

仁王 *niō* [benevolent-king] fierce twin guardian statues

仁者 *jinsha* [benevolent-person] humanitarian

義 *gi*—Justice

主義者 *shugisha* [master-righteous-person] ideologist

正義 *seigi* [correct-righteous] righteousness

義理 *giri* [righteous-logic] social obligation

As an aside, women in Japan will often give chocolates to male coworkers on Valentine's Day called 義理チョコ *giri choko*, or "social obligation chocolate."

礼 *rei*—Courtesy

礼法 *reihō* [courtesy-law] etiquette, manners

礼式 *reishiki* [salute-ceremony] courtesy

失礼 *shitsurei* [lose-courtesy] "excuse me"

礼金 *reikin* [courtesy-gold] a reward

立礼 *ritsurei* [stand-bow] a standing bow

座礼 *zarei* [sit-bow] a seated bow

The bowing and clapping ritual common to some *dōjō* is known as 二礼二拍一礼 *ni rei ni haku ichi rei* ("two bows, two claps, one bow") in Japanese; it originally comes from 神道 *Shintō* practices. Another similar phrase used to describe this is 二礼二拍手一礼 *ni rei ni kashiwade ichi rei* (same meaning). If your *dōjō* ritual happens to involve a different number of claps or bows, feel free to replace those numbers with whatever is appropriate. *Note: In addition to kashiwade,* 拍手 *is also pronounced hakushu, which means "applause."*

智 *chi*—Wisdom

全智 *zenchi* [all-wisdom] omniscience

無智 *muchi* [no-wisdom] ignorance

信 *shin*—Sincerity, Faith, Trust

信号 *shingō* [reliable-number] traffic signal

自信 *jishin* [oneself-faith] self confidence

As a final note, I've heard the notion that the pleats on the front of the 袴 *hakama* (see: Equipment) are supposed to be connected to the Confucian Virtues, with each pleat representing one of the virtues.

7

TRAINING

道場 *dōjō*—The Place of the Way

Training often takes place in a dōjō which comprises many parts. Whether you train in a small 田舎道場 [rice paddy-hut-dōjō] *inaka* (country) *dōjō* , 支部道場 [branch-section-dōjō] *shibu* (branch) *dōjō*, or the 本部道場 [main-bureau-dōjō] *hombu* (headquarters) *dōjō*, you may see similar things.

玄関 *genkan* [mysterious-barrier] entrance

上座 *kamiza* [upper-seat] seat of honor

上席 *jōseki* [upper-place] seat of honor

神棚 *kamidana* [deity-shelf] Shintō shrine

神前 *shinzen* [deity-front] Shintō shrine

仏壇 *butsudan* [Buddha-altar] A Buddhist altar

正面 *shōmen* [true-surface] front (of the dōjō)

畳 *tatami* floor mat

名札 *nafuda* [name-label] wooden plates with dōjō members' names

道場訓 *dōjō kun* [dōjō-instruction] dōjō rules of conduct

Training

The Japanese word 稽古 *keiko* is often translated into English as "training." While this isn't necessarily wrong, I think it's incomplete, as the original word conveys something along the lines of "reflecting on the past" or "considering the old." Let's take a look at the component characters that comprise 稽古:

稽 *kei*—consider, think

稽古着 *keikogi* [keiko-clothing] training uniform

見取稽古 *mitorigeiko* [see-take-keiko] observation

Note: 見学 kengaku [see-study] is also often used to express observing a class.

古 *ko*—old, ancient

古式 *koshiki* [old-style] old style, ancient ritual

古武道 *kobudō* [old-martial-path] ancient martial arts

We often speak of "training" in Aikidō. But to what kind of training are we referring? Study? Research? Observation? Repetitious drilling? The English word "training" alone seems a bit inadequate to describe all of the facets of learning that take place in the dōjō… and elsewhere. Here are some words often used to describe various facets of training.

暑中稽古 *shochūgeiko* summer training

寒稽古 *kangeiko* winter training

年越し稽古 *toshikoshi geiko* New Year's Eve training

越年稽古 *etsunen geiko* [forget-year training] (see *toshikoshi geiko*)

鏡開き *kagami biraki* opening the mirror

稽古初め *keiko hajime* first training of the new year

初稽古 *hatsu geiko* [begin-training] (see *keiko hajime*)

鍛錬 *tanren* [forge-polish] a process of polishing

練習 *renshū* [polish-study] study

訓練 *kunren* [teachings-polish] training, drilling

教訓 *kyōkun* [teach-precept] lesson, precept, moral

訓育 *kun'iku* [teach-upbringing] education, discipline

学習 *gakushū* [study-learn] learning, study

講習会 *kōshūkai* [lecture-study-meet] a conference

研究 *kenkyū* [hone-research] research

合宿 *gasshuku* [together-lodge] lodging together

Strictly speaking, I suppose I could say that if you're not all sleeping together in the dojo, you're not technically having a gasshuku. Again… pedantic. I get it. I really do.

A student who lives in the dōjō and spends most of his or her time training, either with the teacher, colleagues, or solo, can be called an 内弟子 *uchi deshi* or inside disciple, or a 研修生 *kenshūsei*, or (special) research student.

Now that we've talked about different *types* of training, let's talk about the various tools that we, as students of Aikidō, have at our disposal to carry out that training.

At the Iwama dōjō, I often heard the following used to describe their particular modes of training:

固い稽古 *katai keiko* static/hard training

柔らかい稽古 *yawarakai keiko* flexible/soft training

流れの稽古 *nagare no keiko* flowing training

Regarding these modes of training, according to Saitō Morihiro, Ueshiba sensei said:

> 流れの稽古は三段から *nagare no keiko wa sandan kara* "Flowing training starts after 3rd dan."

Kata

The word *kata* is certainly not unfamiliar to most students of martial arts. But did you know that there are two different characters with somewhat similar meanings, both of which are pronounced *kata*? Here's your chance to work out your new kanji chops: Do you see a common radical in both characters?

型—model

制定型 *seiteigata* [law-set-model] set kata

模型 mokei [copy-model] model, maquette

形—form (shape)

形稽古 *katageiko* [model-training]training in kata

護身術の形　*goshinjutsu no Kata* [protect-body-art-kata] self-defense kata

I have heard it claimed that Ueshiba Morihei said that there is no kata in Aikidō. While it may be true that kata (form) is fluid and changing when one is actually *doing* Aikidō, doing is quite different from learning and training. Educationally speaking, kata is an invaluable *training* tool, and it exists in virtually every Japanese art form.

We must also remember that Ueshiba may have been operating on a level beyond his students and may have transcended the notion of systematized kata in his mind. I think it is a mistake to think that imitating what it *looked like* he was doing at his level will necessarily *lead to* that level. So, it has been left to Ueshiba sensei's various students to systematize his teachings so that they might be passed on more efficiently to the future students of Aikidō. This teaching/learning tool is called "kata."

It has also been said that Ueshiba sensei claimed he did not know how to teach Aikidō, and that his students were required to "steal" it from him and find their own Aikidō. Many of his students attempted to systematize his teachings in order to pass them on. To students of the teachings of Tomiki Kenji, the notion of kata training is not at all foreign.

The notion of the uselessness of kata training may also be rooted in the notion that "kata doesn't work." In my experience, this view betrays a fundamental lack of understanding of the very purpose of 形稽古 *katageiko* [kata training]. We learn mathematics, music, language, and countless other skills by following patterns, not by trudging through whatever random, unconnected problems life throws at us.

Some Westerners think of kata as an "choreographed fight against imaginary opponents." Speaking for myself, this notion came from many of the Karate books I read in the 1970s (damn you, Bruce Tegner!). This is, however, incomplete and misleading. Unlike many solo Karate kata, Aikidō uses 相対形 *sōtai kata* [mutual-versus-kata], or kata that involves two opposing participants training together. This sort of kata training is not exclusive to Aikidō, but also occurs in various weapons arts, Jūjutsu, and Jūdō. As Karate kata are generally performed solo, the 分解 *bunkai*, or applications, of those kata can be more difficult to grasp.

How do you know ikkyō when you see it? You know it because of its shape and function. When you practice ikkyō over and over, you're practicing kata. (Whether that kata is set or varies constantly is another issue.) Kata is merely a tool for instilling principles through physical form. Whether you believe that there is or is not—or should or should not be—kata in Aikidō, every time you practice a recognizable technique, you are training in kata, or the form of that technique.

Randori

The component characters of the word 乱取 *randori* are 乱 [chaos, disorder, uprising, disturbance, war] and 取 [take, snatch]. This paints a very vivid picture of the practitioner attempting to steal form from formlessness. I often refer to *randori* as "taking (form) from chaos."

The randori that I imagine most Aikidō people are familiar with takes the form of a lone person facing 2 or more opponents. The randori of Jūdō and Jiyūshin-ryū Aikibudō, however, is quite different. Instead of multiple attackers coming full-speed, this type of randori is done one-on-one in a relaxed, slow manner. In this form of randori, the initiative can switch back and forth as one partner *takes* the initiative from tori, thereby becoming tori him or herself. This exchange continues until it results in a throw or lock.

No matter which picture comes to mind, one thing is common: in order for it to truly be randori, you must be *taking* techniques out of a *chaotic* situation. Randori is designed to complement a system of kata training, bringing the principles learned in kata to life in the form of controlled reality.

There are other training tools we use in Aikidō that do not quite meet the definition of randori (although some people use the terms interchangeably... more on that in a second), but still teach other valuable lessons.

When two people attack one person, it is called 二人掛け *niningake* [two-on-one]. When many (i.e. more than two) attack a single individual, it is called 多人数掛け *taninzūgake* [many-on-one]. Both of these forms of training help teach the lessons of controlling one's space and using one's opponents against each other. Two common strategies taught in these exercises are to use opponents as shields against their allies and to causing them to get in each other's way.

When a student is free to perform whatever technique he or she chooses, rather than being held to only one, it is 自由技 *jiyūwaza* [free technique]. There seems to be, however, a bit of gray area between various dōjō where differentiating between *jiyū waza* and *randori* is concerned. My take is that randori involves jiyū waza, but that jiyū waza does not necessarily share the element of stealing form from "chaos." In other words, I would say that jiyū waza could be a subset of randori. Your mileage may vary.

In training, one will often flow from one technique directly into another when the first fails to yield the desired result. This is often known as 連絡技 *renrakuwaza* [connected-technique]. The specific term used to indicate a change in technique is 変化技 *henkawaza*. Another phrase related to this notion of fluid, continuing movement is 気の流れ *ki no nagare*, or "the flow of *Ki*".

Finally a demonstration of any form of martial skill—like the ones performed at the 全日本合気道演武大会 *zen nippon aikidō embu taikai* All-Japan Aikidō Demonstration—is called 演武 *embu* [performance-military]. A martial arts demonstration performed as an offering, such as the one performed at the Aiki Shrine on the anniversary of Ueshiba's death, is called 奉納演武 *hōnō embu* [offering-demonstration-martial].

~

準備 *jumbi*—preparation

準備体操 *jumbi taisō* [semi-prepare-body-manipulate] preparatory exercises

体操 is a word commonly used for gymnastics and calisthenics

柔軟体操 *jūnan taisō* [flexible-soft-calisthenics] stretching

柔 is the same character used in the arts 柔道 Jūdō and 柔術 Jūjutsu. It is composed of 矛 (halberd) and 木 (tree). Imagine a tree soft enough that you can pierce it with your spear.

動作 dōsa [move-make]—action; movements

運動 *undō* [carry/transport-move] motion, exercise

左右運動 *sayū undō* [left-right-movement] left-right exercise

背伸運動 *haishin undō* [back-lengthen-exercise] back stretching

単独運動 *tandoku undō* [single-alone-exercise] solitary exercises

一人技 *hitori waza* [one-person-technique] solitary technique

八方運動 *happō undō* [eight-direction-exercise] 8 direction movement

八方切 *happō giri* [eight-direction-cut]

深呼吸 *shin kokyū* [deep-inhale-exhale] deep breathing

呼吸法 *kokyū hō* [respiration-law]

呼吸動作 *kokyū dōsa* [respiration-exercise]

素振り *suburi* [elementary-swing] swinging a sword

8

EQUIPMENT

道具 *dōgu* [path-tool] is a generic Japanese word for tools or equipment. If you want to talk specifically about equipment for martial arts, use the word 武道具 *budōgu* [military-path-tool].

Clothing

For decades, I have heard English-speaking practitioners talking about their "*gi*," which they take to mean their training uniform. In 10 years in Japan, and 30 years studying the language, I have never once heard a Japanese person refer to this uniform as a "*gi*." Japanese, being a highly homophonic language, is so rife with homonyms, that using "*gi*" by itself would end up being quite confusing. Here is some terminology that could prove useful, should you find yourself talking to a Japanese-speaking person about your *Aiki Jammies*.

稽古着 *keikogi* [consider-old-garment]—training uniform

It makes sense that the *garment* you wear while *training* would be called 稽古着. Additionally, there are other related terms for training garments:

道着 *dōgi* [way-garment] training uniform

柔道着 *jūdogi* [flexible-path-garment] Jūdō training uniform

合気道着 *aikidōgi* [aikidō-garment] Aikidō training uniform

剣道着 *kendōgi* [sword-path-garment] Kendō training uniform

空手着 *karategi* [empty-hand-garment] Karate training uniform

The 稽古着 can also be broken up into its constituent parts.

上着 uwagi [upper-garment]—jacket

This is the name of the upper jacket that one wears in such arts as *Aikidō, Jūdō, Karate-dō*, and various classical weapons systems. Other parts of the *uwagi* are often used in technique names:

襟 *eri* collar

袖 *sode* sleeve

袈裟 *kesa* a Buddhist monk's robe

Note: 袈裟 is sometimes used in budō to describe the angle at which the robe collar slants (e.g. 袈裟切り *kesagiri* [kesa-cut] or 袈裟固め *kesagatame* [kesa-hold]).

Pants

One might think that since the name for the jacket is 上着 *uwagi*, it would logically follow that the name for the pants would be 下着 *shitagi*. However, logic being what it is, *shitagi* actually means "underwear" (i.e. skivvies). Sorry about that.

The word for the pants that one wears as part of the keikogi is ズボン *zubon*. There are no kanji that I have been able to find for zubon, as it is apparently a Japanization of the French word *jupon* (underskirt, petticoat, slip), and is therefore written using *katakana*.

袴 *hakama*—divided pleated skirt-like pants

Despite the ubiquitous myth that the hakama was designed to obfuscate one's footwork, it actually serves no such purpose. In fact, hakama were a normal part of the daily dress of those who could afford them. Many of Ueshiba's early students reported that he required everyone to wear hakama while training because he thought it disrespectful to show up in front of one's teacher in one's underwear (which is how zubon were seen).

腰板 *koshi ita* [loin/waist-board] stiff trapezoidal board-like section worn in the small of the back

紐 *himo* [string] straps used to tie the hakama. They are two sets: 前紐 in the front and 後紐 in the rear.

袴止め *hakama dome* [hakama-stop] a flat, plastic, spoon-like object attached inside the hakama, under the koshi ita. It is tucked into the belt to prevent the hakama from sagging. Thought by Aikidōka to be potentially dangerous during falls and rolls, they are sometimes absent—or removed—in hakama designed for use in Aikidō. Also called ヘラ *hera*.

帯 *obi*—belt

Belts signifying rank were introduced to Aikidō along with the dan-kyū ranking system. During my time in Japan, I only saw white, brown, and black belts used by adults (children were often allowed to wear other interim colors). Another popular martial arts myth surrounding the significance of the colors chosen for each belt exists. The story goes that the beginner starts with a pure white belt. Through the training process, the belt becomes yellow with sweat, green because of the grass, then brown because of the dirt, etc. This is why many people claim that it is inappropriate to wash one's belt. While it sounds nice, it is, unfortunately, just another myth. Sorry.

Following are some common—and, perhaps, not-so-common—belt

colors that one may see along the path. Note that not all colors are used in every dōjō or style of Aikidō.

白帯 *shiro obi* white belt

黄色帯 *kiiro obi* yellow belt

緑帯 *midori obi* green belt

茶色帯 *chairo obi* brown belt

黒帯 *kuro obi* black belt

紅白帯 *kōhaku obi* red and white belt (6th - 8th dan)

赤帯 *aka obi* red belt (9th - 10th dan)

Weapons

In Japanese, any sort of weapon can be referred to as 武器 *buki* [military-tool] and techniques involving weapons can be called 武器技 *bukiwaza*.

刀 *katana*—curved Japanese sword

木刀 *bokutō* [wood-katana] wooden training sword

短刀 *tantō* [short-katana] knife (short sword)

脇差 *wakizashi* [flank-wear] short sword

太刀 *tachi* [big-katana] large sword with a pronounced curve, worn as a sign of rank, generally blade down.

居合刀 *iaitō* [to be-fit-sword] a (usually dull) sword, designed to be used in the practice of *Iaidō*, or sword drawing. Sometimes referred to as 模擬刀 *mogitō* [copy-imitate-sword].

剣 *ken*—sword

木剣 *bokken* [wood-sword] wooden training sword (Note: I almost never heard this word used in a dōjō in Japan; bokutō was far more common.)

剣道 *kendō* [sword-path] Kendō

丸棒 *marubō*—staff

六尺棒 *rokushakubō* [six-shaku-staff] 6 shaku staff, quarterstaff

A shaku is a traditional Japanese measurement, roughly equivalent to one foot or 30 cm. A rokushakubō, therefore, is about 180 cm—approximately 6 feet—long. Other traditional measurements seen in budō are 寸 sun (1.2 in / 3 cm) and 分 bu (.1 in / .3 cm), often when measuring sword lengths.

半棒 *hanbō* [half-staff] half-length staff

杖 *jō* short staff, cane

As an aside, I sometimes found it difficult to get my point across when visiting 武道具屋 *budōguya* (martial arts supply store) to buy a 杖 (also pronounced *tsue*). I would often instead have to ask for 丸棒 *marubō* (rounded-stick).

銃剣 *jūken* [gun-sword] bayonet

9
THE BODY

体 *karada*—the body

筋肉 *kin'niku* [muscle/sinew-meat] muscle

関節 *kansetsu* [connection-knuckle] joint

関節技 *kansetsu waza* a joint-locking technique

頭 *atama*—head

顔 *kao* face

正面 *shōmen* [true-face] front surface of head

横面 *yokomen* [profile-face] side surface of head

顎 *ago* chin

首 *kubi* neck

喉 *nodo* throat

胴 *dō*—trunk

胸 *mune* chest (also *muna*)

側面 *sokumen* [side-surface] side of body

脇 *waki* armpit, flank

水月 *suigetsu* [water-moon] solar plexus

腹 *hara* abdomen

臍下丹田 *seika tanden* [abdomen-lower-cinnabar-field] the pit of the stomach

臍下一点 *seika itten* [abdomen-lower-one-point] one point

腕 *ude*—arms

腕 *ude* arm

肩 *kata* shoulder

肘 *hiji* elbow

手 *te* hand

小手 *kote* [small-hand] forearm

籠手 *kote* [cage-hand] gauntlet; a forearm protector used in 剣道 *Kendō*

手首 *tekubi* [hand-neck]wrist

指 *yubi* finger

脚 *ashi*—legs

脚 *ashi* leg

腰 *koshi* hip; loin

膝 *hiza* knee

膝行 *shikkō* [knee-go] knee walking

足 *ashi* foot/leg (*If you look closely, you might be able to see a pelvis, tibia, patella, heel, arch, and toes.*)

足首 *ashikubi* [foot-neck] ankle (Do you see a pattern here? Hand neck... foot neck...)

アキレス腱 *Akiresu-ken* Achilles' tendon

姿勢 *shisei*—posture

姿勢 *shisei* [figure-strength] posture; alignment

構 *kamae* posture; stance

自然体 *shizentai* [nature-body] natural posture

自然本体 *shizenhontai* [nature-main-body] natural posture with both feet even (i.e., neither foot forward)

右自然体 *migi shizentai* [right-natural-body] right natural posture

左自然体 *hidari shizentai* [left-natural-body] left natural posture

半身 *hanmi* [half-body] an oblique posture wherein the heel of the rear foot is on the same line as the front foot

一重身 *hitoemi* [one-layer-body] an oblique posture similar to hanmi, but in which the ball of the rear foot is on the same line as the front foot

相 *ai* mutual

相半身 *ai hanmi* matching oblique stance

相構 *ai gamae* matching posture

相打 *ai uchi* simultaneous strike; mutual kill

相抜 *ai nuke* mutual escape; neither party is injured or killed

相手 *aite* partner ("the other party")

逆 *gyaku* reverse, opposite

逆半身 *gyaku hanmi* opposite oblique stance

逆構 *gyaku gamae* opposite posture

安定 *antei* stable

不安定 *fuantei* unstable

Sword Postures

八相の構え (also 八双) *hassō no kamae* [eight-features-posture] figure "eight" posture. This is a reference to the 8 features that characterized the life of Buddha. One of my early teachers taught me that it was called such because of the sideways Japanese 八 "eight" shape that is created between the upraised sword and scabbard. I don't know whether there's any truth to this, but it served as a good mnemonic for me.

上段 *jōdan* upper level

正眼 *seigan* [correct-eye] sword pointed at the opponent's eyes

中段 *chūdan* middle level

下段 *gedan* lower level

脇の構え *waki no kamae* flank posture—the sword is held low and to the rear

Standing and Sitting

立技 *tachi waza* [stand-technique] standing techniques

半身半立 *hanmi handachi* [half-body-half-stand] techniques done in a manner where one person is standing and the other is seated

正座 *seiza* [correct-sit] traditional Japanese seated (kneeling) position

座技 *suwari waza* [sit-technique] seated techniques (also read *zagi*)

安座 *anza* [relax-sit] sitting cross-legged

居合腰 *iaigoshi* [Iai-loin] a posture used when drawing the sword from seiza where one knee remains on the ground, while the other is up.

立膝 *tate hiza* [stand-knee] a ready posture, similar to anza, but with the sole of one of the feet on the floor

FUNDAMENTALS

Principles

Here are a few words used to mean "prinicple" in Japanese:

原則 *gensoku* [primitive-rule] principle; general rule

原理 *genri* [primitive-truth] principle; fundamental truth

理合 *riai* [logic-fit] principle; theory

Let's take a look at how different systems view basic principles.

Tohei Koichi's Principles

Four Principles of Body-Mind Unification
心身統一の四大原則 *shinshin tōitsu no yon dai gensoku*

臍下の一点に心をしずめ統一する *seika no itten ni kokoro o shizume tōitsu suru* — Keep one point ("sink your mind into the one point in your lower abdomen and unify")

全身の力を完全に抜く *zenshin no chikara o kanzen ni nuku* — Relax completely ("completely release all strength from your entire body")

身体の総ての部分の重みを、その最下部におく *karada no subete no bubun no omomi o, sono sai kabu ni oku* — Keep weight underside ("place the weight of all areas of your body in the lowest part")

氣を出す *ki wo dasu* — Extend Ki

Five Principles of Aikidō with Mind and Body Unified
心身統一合氣道の五原則 *shinshin tōitsu aikidō no go gensoku*

氣が出ている *ki ga deteiru* — *Ki* is extending

相手の心を知る *aite no kokoro o shiru* — Know the other person's mind/heart

相手の氣を尊ぶ *aite no ki wo tattobu* — Respect the other person's *Ki*

相手の立場に立つ *aite no tachiba ni tatsu* — Put yourself in the other person's place

率先窮行 *sossen kyūkō* — Lead with confidence

Tomiki Aikidō Principles

崩し *kuzushi* - To cause a structure to crumble, to destabilize a structure. Often incorrectly (in my opinion) translated as "balance break," kuzushi refers to causing a destabilization of the structural integrity of someone's body, causing a collapse or weakening of the structure. If one wants to say specifically "break balance," one adds the word "balance" (i.e. バランスを崩す *baransu wo kuzusu*). 八方の崩し *happō no kuzushi* [eight-direction *kuzushi*] is a posture-breaking exercise done in Jūdō and some styles of Aikidō that are descended from Tomiki Kenji.

作り *tsukuri* - Creating the structure or shape of the technique. In my lineage, kuzushi and tsukuri happen simultaneously.

掛け *kake* - The start of the technique (i.e., the part where your partner falls down and goes "boom"). In my lineage, kake is not something that is done *to* a person, but rather just happens as a result of proper kuzushi and tsukuri.

間合 ma'ai—distance

間合 *ma'ai* [interval] distance between two objects

  遠間合 *tooi ma'ai* [far-ma'ai] far distance

  内間合 *uchi ma'ai* [inside-ma'ai] inside distance

  近間合 *chika ma'ai* [close-ma'ai] close distance

タイミング—timing

先手 *sente* [before-hand] initiative: the upper hand

  後の先 *go no sen* [late-initiative] late timing: responding at the end of an attack

  先の先 *sen no sen* [early-initiative] early timing: responding at the beginning of an attack

  先々の先 *sen sen no sen* [early-early-initiative] early-early timing: responding to the intent behind the attack

方向 hōkō [direction-facing]—directions

前 *mae* front

When used in combination with another character, (e.g. 前方 *zenpō* "forward direction"), 前 is pronounced *zen*.

後 *ushiro* back

When used in combination with another character (e.g. 後方 *kōhō* "backward direction"), 後 may be pronounced *kō* or *gō*.

横 *yoko* side, profile

右 *migi* right

左 *hidari* left

左右 *sayū* [left-right] sideways

斜め *naname* diagonal

Locations

表 *omote* in front of; obverse (coin)

裏 *ura* behind; reverse (coin)

死角 *shikaku* [dead-angle] blind spot

内 *uchi* inside

    内弟子 *uchi deshi* [inside-disciple] a student who lives in the *dōjō*

    内回転 *uchi kaiten* inside rotation

外 *soto* outside

    外弟子 *soto deshi* [outside-disciple] a student who lives outside the *dōjō*

    外人 *gaijin* [outside-person] foreigner

上 *ue* up, upper

    上段 *jōdan* upper-level

上下 *jōge* up and down

上げ *age* lift, raise

合気上げ *aiki age* [aiki-raise]

中 *naka* middle, center

中段 *chūdan* middle-level

中心 *chūshin* center

下 *shita* down, lower

下段 *gedan* lower-level

下品 *gehin* crude, low-class

下げ *sage* drop

合気下げ *aiki sage* [aiki-drop]

動作 *dōsa*—movements

体術 *taijutsu* body art

体捌き *tai sabaki* [body-handling] bodywork

足捌き *ashi sabaki* [foot-handling] footwork

入身 *irimi* entering body

体の変更 *tai no henkō* [body-change-renew] body change

体の変化 *tai no henka* [body-change-change] body change

転換 *tenkan* [revolve-convert] convert; divert

転回 *tenkai* [revolve-round] revolution; rotation

転身 *tenshin* [revolve-body] body turn

螺旋 *rasen* [screw-rotation] spiral; helix

足捌き *ashi sabaki*—Footwork

摺足 *suri ashi* [slide-foot] sliding the feet across a surface

歩足 *ayumi ashi* [walking-foot] normal walking

継足 *tsugi ashi* [following-foot] walking where the rear foot slides up to just behind the front foot, then the front foot slides forward

送足 *okuri ashi* [send-foot] walking wherein the foot in the direction of movement is moved first

膝行 *shikkō* [knee-go] knee walking from seiza

11

ATTACKS

Tori vs. Tori

There are two ways of expressing the word *tori* in Japanese where grabbing/gripping in *Aikidō* is concerned. While different *dōjō* and styles may have a preference of one over the other, I've found that they seem to be used interchangeably. Still, the meanings of the two versions are different and an understanding of each may serve to expand your horizons.

捕 *tori* arrest; seize

片手捕り *katate dori* one arm grab (arrest)

短刀捕り *tantō dori* tantō seizing

太刀捕り *tachi dori* sword seizing

逮捕する *taiho suru* to arrest

Note: suru is a verb that means "make/do" and is also used to turn nouns into verbs.

取 *tori* take

諸手取り *morote dori* grab (take) one arm with two hands

交差取り *kōsa dori* cross-hand take (I've heard this can also be written 交叉, but I have not personally seen this compound used. In fact, Google Japan tries to correct it to 交差 when one attempts to search for it.)

太刀取り *tachi dori* sword taking

杖取り *jō dori* jō (staff) taking

Grabs

片手 *katate* one hand grabs one (of two) arms

両手 *ryōte* grabbing with both hands

諸手 *morote* two-handed grab on one arm

片手捕り *katate dori* seizing one (of two) hands

両手捕り *ryōte dori* seize with two-hands

肩捕り *kata dori* seizing the shoulder

持 *mochi* hold (sometimes used instead of *tori*)

両手持ち *ryōte mochi* grab with two-hands

片手持ち *katate mochi* grabbing one (of two) hands

Hand Strikes

当身技 *atemi waza* [hit-body-technique] striking

拳 *ken/kobushi* fist

正拳 *seiken* [correct-fist] horizontal fist

縦拳 *tateken* [vertical-fist] vertical fist

一本拳 *ipponken* [one-finger-fist] one-knuckle fist

(本 *is a word used for counting long, thin objects*)

手刀 *tegatana* [hand-sword] (also pronounced *shutō*)

突き *tsuki* [thrust] punch, thrust

追突き *oizuki* [following-thrust] punching with the same hand and foot forward

逆突き *gyakuzuki* [opposite-thrust] reverse punch

直突き *chokuzuki* [direct-thrust] straight punch

打ち *uchi* strike, pound

正面打ち *shōmen uchi* strike to the front (surface)

横面打ち *yokomen uchi* strike to the side (surface)

相打ち *ai uchi* mutual kill, simultaneous strike

Foot Strikes

蹴り *keri* kick

前蹴り *mae geri* front kick

横蹴り *yoko geri* side kick

回し蹴り *mawashi geri* roundhouse kick

後ろ蹴り *ushiro geri* back kick

Cutting

切り *kiri* cut

正面切り *shōmen giri* cut to the front (surface)

横面切り *yokomen giri* cut to the side profile (surface)

袈裟切り *kesa giri* diagonal cut

刃筋 *hasuji* the cutting line, the alignment of the blade in relation to the movement of the cut

Decisiveness

寸止め *sun dome* [one-sun-stop] the ability to stop a strike "on a dime"

寸 *sun* - 1/10th of a 尺 *shaku;* slightly larger than 1 inch

決め *kime* decision, decisive. Sometimes translated as "focus," this implies decisive finality.

極 is another character that can also be read "kime," but means "extreme." It is used in the Chinese martial art 太極拳 [taikyokuken] or Taijiquan.

12

TECHNIQUES

受身 *ukemi* [receive-body]

Why am I including ukemi in the chapter on techniques? Because, to me, ukemi is a technique. In fact, it's one of the most—if not the most —important tools in my own personal Budō toolbox. I can count the number of times I've been attacked by a herd of ninja on zero fingers. To count the number of times I've taken an unexpected spill, on the other hand, would require many times that number of fingers. After 残心 *zanshin* awareness, ukemi has saved my bacon far more than any other tool at my disposal.

In grammatical terms, 受身形 *ukemikei* means "passive voice" in Japanese. Some schools of thought in *Aikidō* reflect this passive nature in their ukemi. However, this is not always the case. For example, the ukemi as practiced in Jūdō, Yoseikan Budō, and my art—Jiyūshin-ryū Aikibudō—is far from passive. While it is true that I still receive techniques as uke, I'm neither giving up, nor do I particularly feel defeated. In fact, it's possible—while in the midst of "taking" ukemi— to turn the situation around, steal the initiative, and turn *tori/nage* into *uke*. That said, whatever your teacher tells you is appropriate ukemi in your dōjō is the rule. Listen to your teacher, and please... don't go dragging me into it. That said, here's my $0.02 on the subject.

One translation of ukemi that, frankly, makes me bleed from the eyes is "breakfall." Other versions that I don't care much for are "high fall" and "hard fall." My reasons for this reaction are both linguistic and practical. Done correctly, there should be nothing necessarily (deliberately) high or hard about *ukemi*, even in *sute ukemi*. The word ukemi can also refer to receiving force in any myriad of ways, not just those resulting in a roll or fall. How you specifically define ukemi, of course, will be largely based upon your particular experience and training philosophy. I, personally, often say that falling down or rolling is the last 1% of ukemi.

Here are some ways ukemi is referred to in Aikidō:

前受身 *mae ukemi* forward ukemi

前方回転 *zenpō kaiten* forward direction roll

前方転倒 *zenpō tentō* forward tumble

後ろ受身 *ushiro ukemi* backward ukemi

後方回転 *kōhō kaiten* backward direction roll

後方転倒 *kōhō tentō* backward tumble

横受身 *yoko ukemi* side ukemi

横回転 *yoko kaiten* side roll

捨身 *sutemi* [sacrifice-body] risking one's life

捨受身 *sute ukemi* a sacrifice fall; sometimes called (never by me) a "breakfall"

宙返り *chūgaeri* somersault

技 *waza*—technique

固め技 *katame waza* locking/immobilization technique

関節技 *kansetsu waza* joint technique/lock

> Another kanji that is pronounced the same way, but has different shades of meaning is 業 *waza*, which means work, deed, act, or (Buddhist) Karma. See 修業 *shugyō* under Concepts for more information.

Different systems sometimes have different names for the same technique. For example, what is called 一教 *ikkyō* lesson one/first teaching in Aikikai is called 押倒し *oshi taoshi* "push-topple" in the Tomiki system and 一ヶ条 *ikkajō* "item one" in Yōshinkan. Here are some more examples:

二教 *nikyō* lesson two/second teaching (remember, *nikkyō* is incorrect)

小手回し *kote mawashi* forearm turn [Tomiki]

二ヶ条 *nikajō* item two [Yōshinkan]

三教 *sankyō* lesson three/third teaching

小手捻り *kote hineri* forearm twist [Tomiki]

三ヶ条 *sankajō* item three [Yōshinkan]

四教 *yonkyō* lesson four/fourth teaching

手首押え *tekubi osae* wrist press [Tomiki]

四ヶ条 *yonkajō* item four [Yōshinkan]

五教 *gokyō* lesson five/fifth teaching

五ヶ条 *gokajō* item five [Yōshinkan]

六教 *rokkyō* lesson six/sixth teaching

脇固め *waki gatame* flank lock [Tomiki]

Throws

投技 *nage waza* throwing techniques

入身投げ *irimi nage* entering-body throw

合気投げ *aiki nage* aiki throw [Tomiki name for irimi nage]

小手返し *kote gaeshi* forearm return/turn over (see below)

小手下し *kote oroshi* forearm drop [Ki Society name for kote gaeshi]

四方投げ *shihō nage* four-direction throw (Note: *shihō* in Japanese really means more like "all directions." Think of it as being similar to the English phrase "the four corners of the Earth.")

十字投げ *jūji nage* figure-ten throw

天地投げ *tenchi nage* heaven and earth throw

天秤投げ *tenbin nage* balance scale throw

回転投げ *kaiten nage* rotating/turning throw

隅落し *sumi otoshi* corner drop

十字絡み *jūji garami* figure-ten entanglement

岩石落し *ganseki otoshi* dropping rock throw

肘当て *hiji ate* strike the elbow throw

腰技 *koshi waza* hip technique

足技 *ashi waza* foot/leg technique

手技 *te waza* hand technique

呼吸 *kokyū* breathing in and out; respiration

呼吸投げ *kokyū nage* breath throw

呼吸法 *kokyū hō* breath method (seated kokyū exercise)

呼吸動作 *kokyū dōsa* breath movements (same as above)

呼吸力 *kokyu ryoku* breath power

深呼吸 *shin kokyū* deep breathing

返し *kaeshi* return/turn over

> The character 返 is used in such technique names as 小手返 *kote gaeshi* ("forearm return/turnover") and 返技 *kaeshi waza* (technique) reversal ("return/turn around technique"). In colloquial Japanese, it can be used thus: 金を返せ！ *kane wo kaese!* Give me my money back!

Terms used in Tomiki Aikidō

倒し *taoshi* topple

押し倒し *oshi taoshi* Tomiki Aikidō technique similar to ikkyō

落し *otoshi* drop

前落し *mae otoshi* [front-drop]

隅落し *sumi otoshi* [corner-drop]

押し *oshi* push

抑え *osae* to press/suppress/hold down

引き *hiki* to draw (like a bow-string)

引落し *hiki otoshi* drawing drop

転回小手返し *tenkai kote gaeshi* an old name for shihōnage

腕捻り *ude hineri* arm twist

13

CONCEPTS

禊 *misogi*—purification rituals

祝詞 *norito* [celebrate-words] 神道 *Shintō* ritual prayer

水の行 *mizu no gyō* the practice of meditating under a waterfall

船漕運動 *funa kogi undō* [boat-row-exercise] "boat rowing" purification exercise

振玉運動 *furi tama undō* [shake-ball-exercise] "ball shaking" purification exercise

禊の杖 *misogi no jō* [purification-of-cane] purification ritual with the short staff

精神鍛錬 *seishin tanren* [spirit-forge-polish] spirit forging

三原 *sangen*—three fundamentals

☐ 生霊 *iku musubi* [live-spirit] *vivifying fundamental* (entering)

◯ 足霊 *taru musubi* [foot-spirit] *completing fundamental* (blending)

△　玉 留 霊　*tamatsume musubi* [jewel-fasten-spirit] *fulfilling fundamental* (form)

残 心 *zanshin* [remaining-mind] remaining awareness after the execution of a technique

無我 *muga* [no-self] no sense of oneself

無心 *mushin* [no-mind] no unnecessary thoughts

無構 *mugamae* [no-posture] no set, prescribed stance

誠 *makoto* sincerity

　　忠誠 *chūsei* [loyalty-sincerity] loyalty, fidelity

殺人剣 *satsujin ken* [kill-human-sword] the sword that takes life (also, 殺人刀 *setsunin tō*)

活人剣 *katsujin ken* [save-human-sword] the sword that gives life

言霊 *kotodama* [word-spirit] the soul of language

山彦 *yamabiko* mountain echo

隙 *suki* an opening in one's defense; a chink in one's armor

武産 *takemusu* [martial-birth] spontaneous martial creativity

結び *musubi* a knot

> 気結び *ki musubi* connection / tying a "knot" between one's own and another's "ki"

> 気の流れ *ki no nagare* the flow of "ki"

修行 *shugyō* [study-journey] pursuit of knowledge, training, practice, ascetic discipline (also 修業 *shugyō*)

> 武者修行 *musha shugyō* [warrior-person-study-journey] traveling about to test one's martial skills

出会い *deai* [go out-meet] meeting, encounter, rendezvous

不動心 *fudōshin* [not-move-heart] imperturbable spirit

陰陽 *in'yō* [shadow-light] yin/yang, positive/negative ☯

黙想 *mokusō* [silent-thought] meditation, silent contemplation

悟り *satori* Enlightenment in Zen Buddhism

我慢 *gaman* perseverance, endurance

頑張って *gambatte* Don't give up! (Said to others as an imperative, an admonition.)

Note: The following words can sometimes sound the same to the untrained ear and are sometimes mistaken for one another:

中心 *chūshin* [middle-heart] center; middle

重心 *jūshin* [heavy-heart] center of gravity

守破離 *shu-ha-ri*—three stages of apprenticeship

守 *shu*—protect; obey

In the beginning stages of learning, you must pay strict attention to what your teacher says and does. This is not the stage for creativity and exploration; you should observe your teacher's movement and listen to what she says, then copy her actions and words as exactly as possible. Protect and obey.

Other occurrences of this character include:

お守り *omamori* amulet; charm

子守 *komori* [child-protect] babysitting

守弘 *Morihiro* Japanese male given name (see Saitō Morihiro)

As your teacher starts requiring you more and more to solve your own problems and answer your own questions, you're likely getting close to passing into the next stage.

破 *ha*—tear; break

In this phase of your journey, you not only retain the responsibility for protecting the teachings handed down to you, but also the duty to tear down and break apart everything you've learned. This is when you start to explore possibilities that may not have been explicitly addressed in the lessons you had received up to this point.

Through experimentation, test what you've learned and become the instrument of your own growth.

Other occurrences of this character include:

道場破 *dōjō yaburi* dōjō busting; challenging people at other dōjō to test one's skills

破獄 *hagoku* jailbreak

型破 *kata yaburi* unconventional; breaking the kata

離—*ri* distance

In the final stage, you are free to leave the nest, should you choose to do so. You no longer require a teacher, because you are capable of being your own. You must continue to reflect on the old teachings and transcend the kata while still protecting it for future generations.

Continue to protect your inheritance. Continue to tear it apart.

Other occurrences of this character include:

離婚 *rikon* [separate-marriage] divorce

長距離 *chōkyori* [long-distance-separate] long-distance (i.e. phone call)

電離圏 *denriken* [electric-separate-sphere] ionosphere

The Aiki Shrine

The 合気神社 *Aiki Jinja* was built for Ueshiba Morihei (and later renovated by the Saitō family) across the street from the 岩間修練道場

Iwama Shūren Dōjō—or, simply, *Iwama Dōjō*—to enshrine the deities of Aikidō as Ueshiba envisioned them. Every April 29th, 大祭 *taisai* [big-festival], a festival commemorating the death of Ueshiba Morihei, is held on the shrine grounds, along with 奉納演武 *hōnōenbu* [offering-demonstration-martial] or a ceremonial offering in the form of a small Aikidō demonstration. Many people from all over the world, including very senior teachers, attend Taisai every year.

Post-training at the Aiki Jinja across from the Iwama dōjō with dojomates and friends in the early-mid 1990s. The author is in the back row, center.

14

SONGS OF THE PATH

道歌 *dōka* are poems written for the purpose of conveying a moral or instructive lesson in the 短歌 [short-song] *tanka* style of 和歌 [Japanese-song] *waka*. These songs generally comprise 31 morae in a 5-7 5-7 7 pattern.

While Ueshiba sensei was certainly not the only teacher, poet, or religious figure to leave dōka for others to ponder, for obvious reasons, his are the only ones that I will take a look at in this book. While there are quite a number of Ueshiba's dōka out there, I have only selected a few for this chapter. Those that I have chosen to translate come from various sources, including the book 武産合気 *Takemusu Aiki* and a collection shared by Ueshiba's student and calligraphy teacher, 阿部醒石 *Abe Seiseki*. I have attempted to group a few of them by theme.

I must warn the reader, though. These can be quite difficult to understand without a thorough background in old-ish Japanese, Ueshiba's notions on Aikidō, ancient texts like Kojiki, Shintō, and probably a healthy dose of 密教 *Mikkyō* (esoteric Buddhist teachings) as well. They were quite difficult for me to translate; I can only blame that on my own lack of knowledge and limitations as a translator.

Aiki

As seen in the Aikidō chapter, Ueshiba's concept of Aiki became more rooted in religious mysticism over the years, altering it from its original extant meaning. The following dōka paint a good example of this.

合気とは *aiki to wa*
筆や口には *fude ya kuchi ni wa*
つくされず *tsukusarezu*
言ぶれせずに *iibure sezu ni*
悟り行へ *satori gyō he*

Aiki cannot be expressed with a brush or by mouth
Without saying a word,
On to Enlightenment

合気とは *aiki to ha*
解けばむつかし *hodokeba mutsukashi*
道なれど *michinaredo*
ありのままなる *ari no mama naru*
天のめぐりに *ten no meguri ni*

Aiki is difficult to interpret
Just follow the natural Path of the Heavens

合気とは *aiki to ha*
愛の力の本にして *ai no chikara no moto ni shite*
愛はますます *ai ha masu masu*
栄えゆくべし *haeyukubeshi*

Aiki
The root of the power of love
A love that must increasingly prosper

Mountain Echo

One of my personal favorite themes in Ueshiba's dōka is the notion of
山彦 *yamabiko* Mountain Echo. In fact, I named my first dōjō 山彦道場
Yamabiko Dōjō.

天地に tenchi ni
気結びなして ki musubi nashite
中に立ち naka ni tachi
心構えは kokoro kamae wa
山彦の道 yamabiko no michi

Join your ki with Heaven and Earth
Stand ready in the middle of it all
The Path of the Mountain Echo

火と水の hi to mizu no
合気にくみし aiki ni kumishi
橋の上 hashi no ue
大海原に daikaigen ni
いける山彦 ikeru yamabiko

Stand on the bridge that was built
Through the Aiki of fire and water
In the great deep
Is the Mountain Echo

日土月 hi tsuchi tsuki
合気になりし aiki ni narishi
橋の上 hashi no ue
大海源は ōunabara wa
山彦の道 yamabiko no michi

Sun, Earth, Moon
Becoming Aiki

Atop the bridge above the great ocean
The path of the Mountain Echo

天地人 *tenchijin*
和楽の道の *waraku no michi no*
合気道 *aikidō*
大海原に *daikaigen ni*
生ける山彦 *ikeru yamabiko*

Heaven, Earth, Man
The Path of Harmonious Music
Aikidō
In the great deep lives the Mountain Echo

Takemusu

武産は *takemusu wa*
御親の火水（いき）に *Oya no iki*
合気して *Aiki shite*
その営は *sono itonami wa*
岐美の神業 *gimi no kamiwaza*

Takemusu comes into being
Through Aiki
With Fire and Water
Of the Divine Parents (Izanagi and Izanami)
The Divine Miracle

Kiai

己が身に *ono ga mi ni*
ひそめる敵を *hisomeru teki wo*
エイと斬り *EI to kiri*
ヤアと物皆 *YAA to monomina*
イエイと導け *IEI to michibike*

To the enemy
concealed within
Cut with "EI!"
Accept (receive) with "YAA!"
Guide with "IEI!"

15

PROVERBS

Strictly speaking, not everything you will see in this chapter is necessarily a proper Japanese proverb. Some are 四字熟語 *yoji jukugo*, or Four-Character Idiomatic Compounds. Others are sayings that are more common to Aikidō or budō in general, and may be unfamiliar to everyday Japanese. And some are, indeed, actual proverbs. Either way, these are sayings that, on some level, at least have something to do with the spirit of training in a martial art.

七転び八起き *nana korobi ya oki*
Fall down seven times, get up eight

No matter how many times you fail, keep going. Failure is not only normal in the pursuit of skill, it's pretty much mandatory. Fail often, fail creatively. Then get back up and keep going.

猿も木から落ちる *saru mo ki kara ochiru*
Even monkeys fall from trees

Who is more adept at climbing trees than a monkey? And yet, they sometimes fall out of trees. Even the greatest of experts makes mistakes.

石の上にも三年 *ishi no ue ni mo san nen*
As many as three years on a rock

No matter how cold and uncomfortable the rock is, if you spend 3 years sitting on it, you will eventually warm it up. It takes a while to accomplish some things.

一期一会 *ichi go ichi e*
One time, one meeting

No experience in this life can ever be repeated. No technique can ever be done exactly the same way twice. Every moment is one-in-a-lifetime chance. (Incidentally, this is the Japanese title for the movie "Forrest Gump.")

柔よく剛を制する *jū yoku gō wo sei suru*
Softness will get the better of hardness

Softness is superior to physical strength and rigidity. It is a fact that you will lose strength with age; it's better to learn how to be effectively soft as early as possible.

気剣体一致 *ki ken tai itchi* [spirit-sword-body-one-do]
Ki, sword, and body in agreement

In English, one might say the weapon is an extension of the body. The weapon and body work together harmoniously.

心技体 *shin gi tai* [heart-technique-body]
Mind, technique, body

Similar to the above: body, spirit, and technique are united.

攻防一致 *kōbō itchi*
Attack and defense coincide

Defense and attack are not separate, but rather the same thing. I've often seen this translated into English as "attack and defense are one," something I think might potentially result from a mishearing by non-native speakers of 一致 *itchi* (coincide, agree, match, conform) as 一 *ichi* (one).

真剣勝負 *shinken shōbu* [real-sword-win-lose]
A life-or-death struggle

Something very serious. A battle to the death with real swords.

精力最善活用 *seiryoku saizen katsuyō* [energy-best-application]
Best use of energy

Simply put, don't waste your energy. Also commonly abbreviated 精力善用 *seiryoku zen'yō*.

自他融和共栄 *jita yūwa kyōei* [self-other-melt-harmony-mutual-prosperity]
Mutual benefit and harmonious reconciliation for all

Mutual benefit, both for the self and the other. If only one side benefits, it isn't mutual. Also abbreviated 自他共栄 *jita kyōei*.

遠山の目付 *enzan no metsuke* [distant-mountain-of-eye-attach]
Gaze at distant mountains

Gaze softly, in an unfocused manner, at a point in the distance rather than focusing tightly on your adversary. Note that の is a grammatical particle that indicates belonging or ownership. In most cases, it's easier for the English speaker to think of it as 's (e.g., 植芝の合気道 *Ueshiba no Aikidō* — Ueshiba's Aikidō).

押さば回れ、引かば斜めに *osaba maware hikaba naname ni*
When pushed, turn; when pulled, enter at an angle

This was reportedly coined by Mifune Kyūzō. His teacher, Kanō Jigorō, said "When pushed, pull. When pulled, push." Mifune sensei, it would appear, changed Kanō's phrase because of his understanding of the force-multiplicational nature of rotation and angles. I find this saying very literally applicable to training and use it often with my students.

以心伝心 *ishin denshin* [from-heart-transmit-heart]
Direct heart to heart communication

Direct transmission of thoughts and feelings from one heart to another without needing to use words. This is the highest level of communication between humans.

温故知新 *onko chishin* [warm-circumstance-know-new]
Revisit the old, know the new

Look to the ancient to learn new things. Develop new ideas as a result of studying the past.

正勝吾勝 *masakatsu agatsu* [correct-victory-I-victory]
True victory is victory over the self

Beating others can be tough, but mastering oneself can be extremely difficult. I find this saying to be related in some ways—if coincidentally—to a passage from The Art of War by 孫子 *Sūn Zǐ*: 知彼知己，百戰不殆；不知彼而知己，一勝一負；不知彼，不知己，每戰必殆 — If you know the other and yourself, you will not be in danger in a hundred battles; if you do not know the other but do know yourself, you will win one and lose one; if you know neither the other nor yourself, you will be in danger in every battle.

勝早日 *katsu hayabi* [victory-fast-day]
Day of swift victory

I think of this as an admonition to not mess around. Win instantly at first touch (if not before). Instant, decisive victory.

鎮魂帰神 *chinkon kishin* [tranquilize-soul-return-god]
Calm the spirit, return to the divine

Calm yourself. Slowing your breathing and your mind will bring you closer to unity with the universe (if you're into that sort of thing).

文武両道 *bunbu ryōdō* [literature-martial-both-path]
The path of the scholar and that of the warrior are the same

While they may not *literally* be the same, the path of the warrior has many things in common with other paths such as those of the scholar pursuits, calligraphy, writing, acting, music, dance, the tea ceremony, etc.

万有愛護 *ban'yū aigo* [10,000-exist-love-protect]
Loving protection of all things

To lovingly protect all things is the purpose of Ueshiba's Aikidō.

水の心 *mizu no kokoro* [water's-heart]
Heart like water

To have a heart like water means not only to flow, but also to be powerful while remaining changeable. Is water hard... soft... or both?

Finally, I'd like to leave you with one last saying, one that speaks very loudly to me. It comes from Buddhism, but whether you're a Christian, Muslim, Jew, Atheist, or other non-Buddhist, I invite you to embrace it.

大道無門 *daidō mumon* [big-path-no-gate]
There is no gateway to the great path

If you want to start, start. If you want to learn to play guitar, get a guitar and play. If you want to write, start writing. If you want to get in shape, start exercising. Not only is there no one guarding the gateway to the path... there isn't even a gate. If you want to walk the path, you're already on it.

Get started.

ABOUT THE AUTHOR

Michael J. Hacker is a budōka, student, teacher, musician, writer, linguist, United States Air Force veteran, amateur mad philosopher, and native Iowan. He has spent the bulk of his life nerding out over language and linguistics and has studied French, Russian, Mandarin Chinese, German, and a smattering of other languages in addition to Japanese. (He's still trying to recover from the Tōhoku accent that he apparently acquired during the five years he lived in Aomori Prefecture.)

Photo by Devon Christopher Adams - devoncadams.com

Michael spent a decade—spanning two Emperors, three Presidents, and countless hairstyles—in Japan, training in Aikidō and other martial arts, studying the Japanese language and culture, and earning advanced black belts in tonkotsu ramen.

While in Japan, Michael had the fortune to share the tatami with such luminaries as Ueshiba Kisshōmaru, Ueshiba Moriteru, Shirata Rinjirō, Saitō Morihiro, Nishio Shōji, Isoyama Hiroshi, Donald Moriyama, Saitō Hitohiro, and countless others senior shihan in addition to regularly training with members of the Japan Self-Defense Forces.

Throughout the 1990s, Michael spent many a day and night training, eating, conversing, and sleeping at the Iwama dōjō. In 1998, he relocated to Tempe, Arizona to further his studies with Jiyūshinkai founder C. E. Clark and the students of the Jiyūshinkan.

In addition to being an Honors Alumnus of the Defense Language Institute at the Presidio of Monterey, California, Michael also holds a Master of Arts in Linguistics from Arizona State University. He has worked as a professional linguist and translator for various companies and government agencies and currently teaches at Arizona State University in addition to writing.

Michael holds the rank of 4th dan, Jiyūshinkai, and is an instructor at the Renshinkan in Mesa, Arizona.

Contact Michael at:
talkingbudo.com
michael@talkingbudo.com